Chicago Public Library

REFERENCE

Form 178 rev. 1-94

COVER GIRLS AND SUPERMODELS 1945–1965

Jean Noël Liaut

COVER GIRLS AND
SUPERMODELS
1945–1965

Translated from the French by
Robin Buss

Marion Boyars
London ▪ New York

Published in Great Britain and in the United States
in 1996 by Marion Boyars Publishers
24 Lacy Road, London SW15 1NL
237 East 39th Street, New York, N.Y. 10016

Distributed in Australia and New Zealand by
Peribo Pty Ltd, 58 Beaumont Road, Mount Kuring-gai, NSW

Originally published in 1994 by Editions Fillipacchi under the title
Modèles et Mannequins (1945–1965)
© Editions Fillipacchi 1994
© This translation Marion Boyars Publishers 1996

British Library Cataloguing-in-Publication Data
    Liaut, Jean-Noël
        Cover Girls and Supermodels, 1945–65
        I. Title   II.   Buss, Robin
        659.152

Library of Congress Cataloging-in-Publication Data
    Liaut, Jean-Noël, 1966–
        [Modèles et mannequins, 1945–1965. English]
        Cover girls and supermodels, 1945–1965 / by Jean-Noël Liaut :
            translated by Robin Buss
        Includes bibliographical references and index
        1. Models (Persons)–Biography.   2.   Models (Persons)   I.   Title.
    HD6073.M77L5313   1995
    659.1'52—dc20   95-38097

ISBN 0–7145–2998–2 Original Paperback

The right of Jean-Noël Liaut and Robin Buss to be identified as authors of this work
has been asserted by them in accordance with the Copyright, Designs and Patents
Act 1988.

Typeset in 11½/14pt Nebraska and Erie by
Ann Buchan (Typesetters), Shepperton
Printed by Redwood Books, Trowbridge, Wiltshire

Contents

Introduction

'It was as though Europe had grown sick of bombs and wanted fireworks instead,' Christian Dior recalled in his 1956 memoirs, *Christian Dior et moi* (*Dior by Dior*). 'It was reassuring to see that the vulgar pageantry of black market society was gradually giving way to the more refined pageantry of Society, with a capital S'. And, more than any other sphere of creative activity, it was haute couture that expressed for him this 'ideal of civilized happiness'. It compensated for the austerity imposed by nearly five years of the Occupation, with headline-making collections every season and the emergence of a new aristocracy of great couturiers, fashion photographers, hairdressers and star models, who set the tone, created a sensation and were soon sought out by the traditional aristocrats of birth and money. Here was prestige based on talent and style, and the whole planet rapidly fell for this world, at once brilliant and savage, extravagant and frivolous, in which the extraordinary became ordinary; a world of frothy chiffon and glossy paper, behind the façade of which were businessmen dealing in millions. No wonder it attracted the curiosity of the intelligentsia: Alice B. Toklas led the way in 1946 with an essay on Pierre Balmain, *A New French Style*, closely followed by John Steinbeck, who wrote the commentary for a short film on the subject of the Paris Collections made for New York television by the great reporter Robert Capa.

It was also immediately after the Liberation that for the first time the profession of 'model', until then the object of hostile prejudice, caught the public imagination. Such women became ambassadors for French prestige, the muses of great designers and photographers, and were thought to live easy and glamorous lives before marrying some famous man: role-models, in short, for several generations of women. And where could one find the clearest evidence of this new infatuation? In the cinema, of course. A popular art by definition and the yardstick of our passions and fantasies, it was the easiest way for all those who did not belong to the élite of society to escape from everyday reality into dreams: from *Cover Girl* (1944) — the title is self-explanatory — to *Blow Up* (1966), a masterpiece by Antonioni, via *Falbalas* (1945), *Mannequins de Paris* (1956), *Funny Face* (1957), the *Nathalie* series (1957 and 1959), in which Martine Carole played a supermodel and detective, down to *Qui êtes-vous Polly Magoo?* (1965). The list is far from exhaustive.

The press began to follow every move made by the models, who also became the subject of bestselling novels, such as Franck Marshall's *Nathalie princesse mannequin de Paris* and its sequels, two of which were later turned into films, and many television documentaries. Their prestige was such that they inevitably attracted the attention of prominent men: aristocrats, opinion formers and famous artists. So it was that Fiona Campbell-Walter married Baron Thyssen; Jean Dawnay, Prince Galitzine; Sophie, Anatole Litvak; Eliette, Herbert von Karajan; and Bronwen Pugh, Lord Astor. A list of such marriages would easily fill several pages and, while liable quickly to become tedious, it would speak volumes. In any event, the palm must undoubtedly go to the magnificent Anglo-Indian, Nina Dyer, who married — one after the other — Baron Thyssen and Prince Sadruddin Khan. However, her suicide in the early summer of 1965 revealed, for the first time, a far more complex reality: the possibility that there might be cracks in the smooth, shiny surface. As time went on, many other models and super-models would become, in turn, the distraught victims of their own success.

The second half of the 1960s witnessed the slow decline of haute couture: the arrival of ready-to-wear, the end of the great fashion houses and hence a new definition of the model's profession. This situation reflected the conflicts and contradic-tions of a society undergoing a political, social and cultural identity crisis. A whole way of life was being challenged. Until the end of the fifties, Paris had been the undeniable cultural capital of the world. Now, little by little, London and New York were taking over and imposing an excessive glorification of youth through rock music, cinema — and fashion. The new models reflected this change in aesthetic standards: the ideal of a sophisticated adult woman gave way to a vogue for child-women, with Twiggy, Penelope Tree, Marisa Berenson and Patti Boyd leading the field, dressed either as cosmonauts by Courrèges, or as metal and plastic flowers by Rabanne, or simply as active, healthy 'Chelsea girls', in mini-skirts by Mary Quant.

PART ONE

COVER GIRLS

Introduction

'I shall not quickly forget the day when one of those specialists in beautiful immobility tried to join a show on the catwalk: a stiff gait, dead arms and huge feet — an absolute disaster!', recalls Freddy, one of the great fashion show models or mannequins, in her memoirs, *Dans les coulisses de la haute couture parisienne.* The story also serves to reveal the immense gap between the work of a catwalk model and a photographic one. For the first, all that really matters is ease of movement, a graceful walk and the ability to give life to a dress in the course of a show. Many of these fashion house models had far from perfect features or ideal bodies. Pierre Balmain humorously recalls one in Liane Viguié's *Mannequin haute couture*: 'There was no shape to her legs and her body was perfectly straight, without hips, waist or breasts. Her pallid face, under her platinum hair, harboured a pair of eyes encumbered with layers of thick sooty make-up above a triple row of false eyelashes. But as soon as she began to walk, her neck stretched slightly forward, with a nasty look in her eye and almost mechanical gestures, she became the very essence of Parisian chic'. In contrast, a cover girl must be, above all, photogenic with a face which catches the light, harmonious outlines and a sense of arrested movement. Of course, some famous models — and there are many of them, from Bettina to Capucine, including Sophie, Simone d'Aillencourt, Denise Sarrault and Ivy Nicholson — were eagerly invited by the great dressmakers to show off their collections, being as much at ease on the catwalk as in a photo session. In the same way, some famous house models, like Marie-Hélène Arnaud, Hiroko Matsumoto, Marie-Thérèse or Victoire, had modelling careers to rival those of the best-known cover girls.

Fashion photography in the 1950s and the first half of the following decade, had its own codes. It became a major art form when dealing with the leading women's magazines or an advertising campaign for the most prestigious designer labels; and a minor, but still essential one, when a model posed for sales catalogues, the popular press or calendars. This book is concerned only with their work in the first of these two categories.

What was the common denominator of all fashion photos intended for the up-market press? Sophistication, ever present in make-up, hair style, gesture, settings and, of course, clothes. What was the height of elegance during this period? A disdainful beauty and an air of distinguished boredom — quite the contrary of the movie stars of the period who, apart from a few like Audrey Hepburn and Kay Kendall, had to be sexy from head to toe; Brigitte Bardot, Sophia Loren and Marilyn Monroe were the epitome of this search for perfection. However, there are as many degrees of sophistication as there are great models: a whole world separates the timeless appeal of Denise Sarrault, which has lost none of its force and still sets a standard even today, and the verve of Sophie, which is very much tied to a particular moment in the history of fashion. Ten years earlier, or five years later, it is quite probable that Sophie would not have enjoyed anything like the same success. She was very much a woman of a particular period. There is an obvious paradox in this bias towards sophistication. The women who read these magazines were supposed to be able to recognize themselves and so identify with these inaccessible creatures; and this, naturally, was far from being the case, even for most of the very rich customers of the great couturiers. However, fashion — and above all haute couture, that artificial, reinvented and impenetrable world in which there is no place for mundane, everyday life — has a unique appeal to fantasy; an irreplaceable dream-like power. Little by little, the concept of sophistication developed. The static poses, ethereal models and theatrical gestures of the early fifties gave way to freedom of movement, aerial grace and natural settings as the decade progressed, reaching its apogee in the healthy, natural woman of the late 1960s, having moved as far as can be imagined from the area dealt with in this book.

Models have often been likened to actresses. For some photographers, every shot was a veritable story in itself, dramatic or comic according to the mood of the moment. The model, who acted out these mini-dramas, changed her mood according to requirements. However, the very elegance of the clothes imposed strict limitations on the range of parts. Unlike actresses, models offered only four or five female stereotypes: the young debutante, the woman of the world, the vamp or the go-ahead, modern young woman, each type could only extend to one or two variants. This is why the the models' 'aura' was essential to individualize every photo.

Nowadays, the press reflects the daily life of the top models, so that the general public has become familiar with a quite separate universe, where people talk about folders, press books and *composites*, a model's 'visiting card', containing a selection of her best photos and her measurements. Forty years ago, there were hardly any agencies and most 'girls' would arrange their own schedules, even though Eileen Ford in New York, Lucie Clayton in London and, from the late 1950s, Dorian Leigh in Paris, had already started to manage the careers of some of them. This was a much less mercenary age, when salaries, especially in France and Britain, were often very modest. Little by little, during the sixties and seventies, things came into focus: the use of agencies became widespread, and there were precise rates for every type of contract and 'Sed cards' (invented by one Sebastian Sed, and the ancestor of *composites*). Models had become businesswomen managing their share portfolios and investing in property.

The United States

Dovima

Dorothy Juba's life is like a fairy story, but one with a nightmare quality. The American Dream in all its inhumanity; or, how the daughter of a Polish cop from Queens, one of the poorer districts of New York, came to represent the Fifties ideal of sophisticated elegance, before lapsing into decline and obscurity.

When still a little girl, Dorothy was delicate and sickly. Constantly weakened by some illness or other, she could not attend school in the normal way and spent seven years without leaving home. What fate could be more unusual? Adored by her mother, an Irish woman who had once been a model, she spent this whole period in a world of dreams that was unique to her, devoting her time to painting, reading and solitude: a contemplative childhood and adolescence.

However, the outside world was soon to sweep her off her feet. In 1949 she was walking down Lexington Avenue when a woman on the staff of *Vogue* came up and invited her into the famous magazine's offices. Shortly afterwards she was making her modelling debut at a photo session with Irving Penn. A promising start, to say the least. By refusing to smile (to hide her teeth, because she considered them less than perfect), she instantly created the image of melancholic, ethereal beauty which was to be her hallmark from then on. When Penn asked her name, she thought back to her childhood and to all those years of seclusion when she had spent her days painting, signing her pictures with the first two letters of her three first names: DOrothy VIrginia MArgaret. Another source has it that only 'Do' really corresponded to the abbreviation of her first name; 'Vi' stood for 'Victory', which had always been her goal; and as for 'Ma', it was a tender reference to her 'Mother'. Whatever the truth may be, the whole world would soon come to know her as 'Dovima'.

In a few months she had appeared on the covers of *Vogue*, *Glamour*, *Harper's Bazaar* and *Ladies' Home Journal.* By 1950, she was earning the record salary — for a top model — of $30 an hour. Letters from admirers would arrive from the whole world, mostly addressed to the magazines, but with no name, just her photograph stuck on the envelope. With her swan-like neck, her finely shaped features and her small bones, Dovima, by a perfect osmosis, became the quintessence of the devastatingly haughty elegance of Balmain, Dior or Fath. She was soon earning $60 an hour, gaining the nickname of 'the dollar-a-minute girl'. She was courted by a number of famous and attractive men, including Ali Khan. A Kashmiri prince wanted to buy her at any price, to make her the jewel of his harem. It was even rumoured that a disappointed suitor had tried to hang himself with one of her silk stockings. But Dovima rejected them all with indifference and without regret.

Throughout these years, the real man in her life was a photographer, the legendary Richard Avedon. They had an unbeatable 'Muse-and-Mentor' act. Thanks to her, he could make his photographs more than just perfectly formed images; he could breathe life and feeling into them. Their collaboration produced some of the most beautiful photographs in the history of fashion, such as 'Dovima and the Elephants'. Shot in 1955 at the Cirque d'Hiver in Paris, during the collections, it shows Dovima standing between two elephants in a fur from Dior designed by the very young Yves Saint Laurent. According to Martin Harrison, this photo finally achieved a satisfying solution to the 'elegant model and cumbersome animal' formula, which had been attempted without notable success by Avedon's predecessors. In the forties, Munkacsi and Louise Dahl-Wolfe had both tried to use elephants as accessories, but in a rather unconvincing way. The reason for their failure was their inability to find any relationship between the grace of the model and the sheer mass of the pachyderm. But Avedon's Dovima, with one hand resting casually on the elephant's trunk while the other is disdainfully held out, succeeds triumphantly in this delicate stylistic exercise. The long evening dress, by Dior, is photographed with sinuous elegance, and the heavy elephants, with the rough leather of their skins, make the perfect foil. It is a miracle of grace and balance, the two trunks harmonizing with the movement of her arms in a delicate series of curves. The picture appeared in *Harper's Bazaar* and was typical of the taste of the period for photos showing models with animals. Thus, Dovima posed with a dalmatian in a matching spotted dress, or as a Parisian woman, dressed by Balenciaga, on the terrace of the Deux-Magots, with a greyhound.

Dovima saw Avedon as a twin brother. She guessed everything that he wanted her to do without him having to explain it. The photographer's fertile imagination reinvented and sublimated her for each new season: Dovima arriving at Maxim's in a dress by Patou*, Dovima in front of the pyramids at Giza wearing an evening wrap by Brooke Cadwallader. For them, the whole planet was merely a huge playing field on which they could display their favourite heroine as they wished. The result was that Dovima was soon unable to distinguish fiction from reality. She became wholly a prisoner of her glossy image, so that even

---

*The photograph appeared in the American *Harper's Bazaar* in October 1955 (p. 133) — a special number on the Paris collections which illustrates the genius of the couple, Avedon and Dovima, in dozens of pictures.

when she was spending an afternoon with some close friends, she had to wear her flawless cover girl make-up. She never realized that she could be loved for herself, not merely for her dazzling appearance between the covers of magazines.

From a professional point of view, her life was stimulating, to say the least. The young woman worked a lot with Avedon, but also posed no less successfully for Cecil Beaton, Horst and Henry Clarke. The last of these knew just how to penetrate the complexity of her personality and bring out her theatrical beauty: whether he was photographing her at the Crillon, at Carlos de Beistegui's or at the Musée de l'Orangerie in front of Monet's 'Water Lilies' for her first appearance on the cover of French *Vogue*, wearing a dress by Dior. She always appeared grave and distant, an extraterrestrial, pristine, lost, forever haunted by some longing for a vanished land. Haute couture and tragic heroines have always suited one another perfectly. Did this, perhaps, reflect a chaotic private life? Dovima certainly had a talent for collecting destructive men. Her first two marriages were a disaster. Her first husband was an alcoholic, the second a brute, inclined to exceptional violence. He would regularly beat his wife, leaving her disfigured for days on end. However, she had willingly married him because he protected her from having to face up to attacks from the outside world, the ups and downs of everyday life and to other domestic problems. It was during this troubled period that she left Eileen Ford and set up her own model agency, *Plaza Five*, where she took on young women like herself, enigmatic and sophisticated beauties. With the coming of the 1960s, Dovima's fame slowly declined. She did not correspond to the new decade's more accessible and natural model of femininity. Her marriage, based on the size of her income as a cover girl, followed the same downward path as her career. Her relationship with her husband deteriorated to such an extent that she decided to run away with their daughter, Allison. He had her prosecuted for abduction and obtained custody of the child in the divorce proceedings. He subsequently set the child against her mother, and, in time, Dovima's letters to her daughter would come back unopened and unread.

She officially retired in 1962, after a brilliant twelve-year career. She then decided to turn to the cinema. Five years before, at the height of her fame, Dovima had appeared in *Funny Face*, the cult film by Stanley Donen, alongside Fred Astaire, Audrey Hepburn and Kay Thompson, as well as other famous cover girls such as Susy Parker and Sunny Harnett. She brought a lot of humour to the role of Marion, a hilarious caricature of a great model. The experience had been good fun, particularly as Richard Avedon was involved as visual adviser on the movie. So, why not go for it and really try to make a career in the cinema? After a few bit parts in TV serials, however, she lapsed into obscurity. It was the start of a period when she lived mainly at night, going out every evening, drinking and smoking to excess, and slowly but surely undermining her already precarious state of health.

In the late 1960s and early 1970s, she drifted from one job to another: secretarial work in model agencies, sales assistant, representative for a cosmetics firm etc. Living in borrowed apartments, she was often too ill to go to work. At this time, she also returned to writing, one of the creative activities of her childhood, dreaming of heroines who were the spitting image of herself. In 1984 she found a job as hostess in a pizzeria in Fort Lauderdale, Florida, where she had gone to live to be near her parents. She also enjoyed her only few years of marital happiness with her third husband, a barman, who died prematurely in 1986. Alone and penniless, Dovima in turn succumbed, to cancer: the most exquisite of the great 1950s cover girls died in May 1990 at the age of sixty-three.

Lisa Fonssagrives-Penn

One day in 1936, in a lift in Paris, Lisa Fonssagrives met a man who invited her to pose for him. Exhausted (she had just given a dancing lesson), but intrigued, because she knew nothing about fashion photography, the young woman accepted. The stranger was none other than Willy Maywald. Shortly afterwards, when they saw the photographs, the editors of French *Vogue* asked her to do a test series with Horst. The rest is history. From that time onwards, until the mid-1950s, Lisa was the favourite model of some of the greatest photographers in the business: Erwin Blumenfeld, Hoyningen-Huene, Louise Dahl-Wolfe, Norman Parkinson and, above all, Irving Penn, who had at last found in Lisa a face of such purity as to be the ideal reflection of his austere pictorial aesthetic. For his camera, she was transformed with disconcerting ease into a siren, a harlequin or an odalisque — the different aspects of one single woman, the inimitable Lisa.

Lisa had been painting, sculpting and dancing since she was a child in Sweden, encouraged in her artistic ambitions by her cultured parents. Art was everywhere in her family, and even her school holidays were spent travelling around Europe to visit museums. As a teenager, she decided to concentrate all her energies on one single field, dancing. Her dream was to work with the famous choreographer Mary Wigman. No sooner said than done. She set off for Berlin to become a pupil of Wigman's, dancing, principally, but also studying sculpture and history of art. Throughout her life she would enjoy the benefit of this ideal period of further education. On her return to Stockholm, she set up a dancing school, able at last to pass on everything that she had studied with such passion herself. Shortly afterwards, while taking part in a competition in Paris with the famous dancer Astrid Malmborg, she fell in love with the city and decided to settle there in order to study other forms of expression besides modern dance. Thanks to Princess Egorova, she was able to acquire a foundation in classical ballet that would have an enduring influence on her posture. At this time, she also met Fernand Fonssagrives, her first husband. He too was a dancer and they both gave lessons from their home.

The day after her test session with Horst, Lisa was posing in a selection of the finest dresses by Alix and Lucien Lelong, at the request of French *Vogue.* In other words, she had stepped directly into the very exclusive company of the great models of the 1930s: Margot Taylor, Helen Bennett, Doris Zelenski, Toto Koopman, Peggy Leaf and that temperamental Russian, Lud. As a model, Lisa considered her poses as arrested dance movements. This choreographic approach to her work was wonderfully successful, combined as it was with a genuine understanding of every outfit. She always tried to put herself in the place of the women who would be wearing the clothes, creating personality through the stylized attitudes of a dancer. This amazing model, a director as much as an actress, was bound to stimulate the imagination of the most demanding fashion photographer: Erwin Blumenfeld, who in 1937 transformed her into a 'daughter of the wind' lost at the summit of the Eiffel

Tower, her striped muslin dress floating like a banner; Hoyningen-Huene who, for *Harper's Bazaar* in 1938, saw her as the double of Pauline Borghese; and Horst, who traced the letters of the word 'Vogue' with her body in 1940. For her, every photo was a new role and an empty stage on which the dancer she continued to be could express herself. During the war, Lisa went to New York and was separated from her husband. Her curiosity was insatiable. Even while continuing to model, she became a photographer in her own right for *The Ladies Home Journal*, developing and printing her photos in a room in her apartment which she had transformed into a laboratory.

When Lisa met Irving Penn in the late 1940s, he had successively been art director and war correspondent before taking up fashion photography, and establishing himself as a master in the field. He was also the only person to create 165 covers for *Vogue* (all editions). The young woman soon became a fixture in his Fifth Avenue Studio (nicknamed 'The Hospital' by his assistants and fashion editors). Their complex personalities were in perfect harmony, both on the professional and personal levels. Penn, a man of silence and concentration, was ideally suited to appreciate her sense of introspection and her liking for solitude — she loved the dark, interminable Swedish winter — as well as her instinctive feeling for nature. Their photos express the full extent of this rare understanding. Each one reveals visual choices informed by exceptional intelligence. Apparently simple, they were in fact the product of great sophistication, in which each line and outline of the body had been judiciously considered, to make a structured image with a respect for volume; the outcome of a cold and dramatic aesthetic. Penn's signature is unforgettable. Hence the photo he took of her in September 1950 for *Vogue* USA in a Marcel Rochas fur, its elegant fluidity suggesting the body of a siren, remains an absolute point of reference. In this portrait, Penn, a perfect master of the language of light and shade, managed better than ever before to play subtly on the sometimes aggressive contrast between them. Lisa, blond, pale and inaccessible, is squeezed in this black velvet vice, with a taffeta fan for its tail and the bust covered in leaves, embroidered in black sequins — shiny and fragile, like dragonfly wings — which forever symbolizes haute couture in the postwar period. Penn photographed her in clothes which marked a high point in the history of women's fashion — the external manifestation of an ideal that was both moral and aesthetic — at a specific moment in our century. It is therefore not surprising that he was the photogapher who best immortalized the clothes of the most illustrious designer of the fifties, Cristobal Balenciaga, whose austere creations were more akin to architecture than to the frivolity of Parisian styles and which, for this very reason, admirably suited the refined sobriety of his photographic world. Who better than Lisa to represent the Balenciaga woman? From his masterpiece, the scarf top in fine linen, to an amazing dress in scalloped chiffon petals, wrapping itself around the body, she was never more elegant than when she was dressed by the Spanish master. Predictably enough, three years after they met at the exhibition, 'Twelve Famous Photographers', Lisa became Mrs Irving Penn. Fiction had merged with reality. From time to time, as if to illustrate the serene happiness of their life together, Penn put aside the distant, icy beauty of black and white and photographed her in colour. Lisa, relaxed and smiling, reading Gertrude Stein's *Picasso* while lying in a field of yellow flowers on Long Island, a fox terrier resting at her side . . . who would have thought it?

In the mid-1950s, while taking drawing classes at the Art Students League, Lisa began to design clothes; at first, a dress now and then in the context of a photo session for her husband, then some evening wear for her elegant friends and, finally, a line in indoor clothes at the request of the department store, Lord and Taylor. She dreamed up delicate lingerie which made women look like ballerinas — in her own image. Striped kimonos in caramel-coloured chiffon, 'Empire' nightdresses in slate-coloured shantung, white and apricot taffeta *déshabillés*: harmony in colours, materials and movements. She sometimes agreed to pose for magazines wearing her own designs: who could resist such a persuasive advertisement?

After six years, the Penns settled down in their Long Island house, a red-painted wooden 'farm' (which grew only flowers). From then on, Lisa had to abandon fashion design. While bringing up her two children, she spent most of her time in her sculpture studio. To her mind, the idea of art was something that had to be understood in a multidisciplinary sense. She had been successively a dancer, model, photographer and designer; but she had also followed classes in psychiatry at Columbia University, devoured Ibsen, Dostoyevsky and Mallarmé as well as the Swedish poet Gustav Fröding and always greatly admired Henry Moore, Picasso and Boccioni (one of the leading figures in Italian Futurism). Her sculpture showed evidence both of her training as a dancer and her work as a model. A feeling for movement and mass, an understanding of light and space: these were the passions of her life. She would also leave her studio to accompany her husband on his frequent travels. In this way, with an assistant and a mobile studio, they journeyed around Dahomey (now Benin), Nepal, Cameroon, New Guinea and Morocco. This allowed Irving Penn to photograph human kind in all its diversity, from the Makebuku warriors of Asaro to the Guedra dancers of Goulimine: a fascinating experience, both in human and in creative terms.

Lisa always said that she had had three lives, each one as rich as the others. Sweden, symbol of her childhood, of purity, of fairy stories and hope of things to come; France, which had given her culture, an awareness of her privileges and maturity; and finally the United States, whose modernity and efficiency had moderated her tendency to dream. She even learned to fly a plane. For her, death was nothing, merely the start of a new cycle; yet her passing, in 1992, left all those who loved her inconsolable.

Dorian Leigh

Her modelling career began with a misunderstanding. One day in 1945, after applying to *Vogue* for a job in the publicity department, she arrived for an appointment with the editor at the magazine's famous New York office, 420 Lexington Avenue, and without quite knowing why, eventually found herself staring into the lens of John Rawlings' camera. The staff had confused her with the model who was expected for a photo session! Dorian good-humouredly went along with the mistake, convinced that it would not lead anywhere. She was wrong. A few days later, Horst launched her career by photographing her for *Time Magazine* as a living incarnation of modern, postwar American youth. In a few months dozens of newspapers and magazines throughout the world were putting her picture on their covers or front pages. Until her retirement at the end of the following decade to set up her own model agency, Dorian was one of the most sought after and best paid models of her time, earning up to 200,000 francs a week in 1955.

Paris, 12 Rue Jean-Goujon. Like all the large mansions in the capital, the Hotel San Regis was famous for its tranquil luxury. Its usual clientele was cosmopolitan, demanding and discrete. But twice a year, in February and August, this elegant calm was shattered by the arrival, from all the corners of the world, of the shock troops of the fashion world: buyers, editors of the most celebrated women's magazines, models and photographers all meeting for the season's collection. The choice of the San Regis was not fortuitous. A few houses further on, at No. 15 in the same street, was the studio of the famous magazine *Harper's Bazaar* which Hemingway in 1935 had called 'the European capital of all the vanities'. For years, *Vogue* and *Harper's* had been competing fiercely in the eyes of the world to become the incarnation of the height of fashion. Although Dorian Leigh had often worked for both of them, she frequented most of all the pages of *Harper's*. She was one of the favourite models of Carmel Snow (the fashion editor whom Paul Valéry described as 'a Louis XV chilblain') and of Richard Avedon, a genius of fashion photography. In her memoirs, *Model Girl*, the great model Jean Dawnay recalls the two of them admiringly: 'I often got the chance to watch Avedon and Dorian working together, which taught me more than any other experience in photographic modelling. They were a perfect team. Avedon would perform antics like a monkey behind his camera, expressing the feelings and miming what he wanted, to which Dorian would respond immediately. She was as mobile and sensitive as a cat, and looked as exquisite as Chinese porcelain with her delicate bones, pale skin and cloud of dark hair.'

Dorian could wear an evening dress by Dior with as much ease as a Balmain suit. She was not very tall but she had long legs and a well-proportioned figure which made her look as if she had been shaped by a sculptor. However, Dorian was not just beautiful to look at. Like all great models, she possessed a good deal of humour, subtlety and psychological insight, often anticipating what photographers wanted of her and charming them by her readiness to do it. In fact, Dorian was much more than a mere cover girl with exceptional attributes: unusually, she had pursued a rich and varied career before entering the world of fashion. Who would have guessed that, during the war, this graduate of Randolph Macon (the smartest school in Virginia, where Pearl Buck was a pupil), had worked as an engineer for the American Army? The only woman in a team of eighty, she drew plans and designed parts and tooling for Wild Cats, the fighter planes built by General Motors! Less surprisingly, every fashion photographer was a fan of this multi-talented young woman who inspired them to greater and greater achievements. She was Avedon's first famous model, right from 1948. He featured her in one of the famous Revlon campaigns, in a scarlet dress with a white fox fur, casually lying beside a huge bowl of blood red cherries matching her make-up . . . Then came Beaton, Sieff and Horst, as well as Irving Penn, who made some of his most individual photographs with Dorian. Like the variation on the theme of beauty and its foils, she posed in the September 1947 issue of *Vogue* (France) in a long lace dress and broad-brimmed hat on the arm of a fat man, who was naked to the waist! Three years later, Penn turned again to Dorian — in a portfolio of work much more original than a mere reportage on a fashion collection — to show off costumes going back to the war years, borrowed from the Metropolitan Museum Costume Institute for the January 1950 issue of *Vogue* USA. There is also Penn's famous self-portrait, in which he appears with the greatest photographers of the day, in a set reminiscent of Courbet. Dorian was the only woman alongside Serge Balkin, Cecil Beaton, George Platt-Lynes, Constantin Joffe, Horst P. Horst, John Rawlings, Erwin Blumenfeld and, of course, Penn himself in the September 1947 edition of French *Vogue.* Her inclusion needs no comment. One might also mention that Dorian came at the start of Henry Clarke's career. While he was an assistant at *Vogue* (USA), preparing backgrounds for in-house photographs, he was present at a photo session in which Dorian posed for Cecil Beaton. Fascinated by the magic of the moment, he decided to take up fashion photography, which he did, with the success we all know. He would later often work with Dorian*, who became a personal friend.

---

* The cover of his book *L'Elegance des années 50 photographiée par Henry Clarke* (Herscher 1986), showed Dorian in a dress by Jacques Heim (1955): a nod to his debut, or mere chance?

The young woman was just as successful after she stopped modelling. Originally, *Vogue* offered her a job as editor in its beauty department, assuring her that she would not have to write a line; someone else would take care of that for her. But she refused to trade solely on her reputation and answered curtly that a model was quite able to write articles! She had been writing since she was in her teens and some of her poems had even been published in the *New Yorker*. In any event, the job didn't appeal to her. Rather than the easy way, she preferred to take on a real challenge. Arriving in Paris for the first time with Avedon in 1949, Dorian appreciated French culture so much that she settled there for good after 1955. Two years later, having decided to end her modelling career in order to marry a Spanish aristocrat, a racing driver, she tried to open a model agency. But, in the late fifties, agencies of this kind were forbidden under French law, since the police were convinced that they could only serve as a cover for organized prostitution. Despite that, Dorian went ahead unhestitatingly. As one might have expected, there was trouble from the very start: a stream of police raids and visits from labour ministry inspectors or tax men. It was a nightmare! Under some antiquated law, people were not allowed to run exployment agencies or to collect a more or less open commission on an employee's income. As a result, the famous Dorian Leigh was threatened with between ten days and three months in prison, and a fine of 50,000 to 300,000 francs. Quite determined to carry on, Dorian went to court in an attempt to change the law once and for all with the help of an energetic young lawyer, Maître Robert Badinter. With remarkable tenacity, which she attributed to her Scottish ancestors (her grandmother, after spending ten years as a prison warder in San Antonio, Texas, had been appointed sheriff of the same town and never hesitated to use her Colt 38 to restore order), she eventually triumphed, persuading the court that the work of a model was a new type of employment not provided for by the law. Moreover, her future agency would offer undeniable protection to young women, many of whom were foreigners, finding their bearings in a new country and unable to speak the language. Finally, Dorian managed to demonstrate convincingly that their work was essential to the

Paris fashion industry, so France had every interest in changing the law. The law bowed before logic and sheer obstinacy, and the case made legal history.

As a result, it is fair to say that Dorian and her family made a considerable contribution to the world of fashion. Her father, George Lofton Parker, helped to improve the quality of colour in high quality photographs. Later, two of the Parker girls, Dorian and Susy, became world famous models. And, not content with this, the young woman had now become the first person to set up an international model agency in Paris, in a small ground-floor office, in a lane near the Trocadero. Under its aegis, she gave work to the greatest cover girls — from Enid Boulting to Wilhelmina, via Denise Sarrault and Maria Solar — a total of 45 models under exclusive contract — and more than a hundred during the collections — for whom she obtained up to 15,000 francs an hour for posing, a quite exceptional amount for the period. Herself the mother of five children (T. L. Hawkins, Marsha, Young, Kim and Miranda), Dorian smothered her protégées with maternal love. All of them gave her their absolute confidence, knowing that her intuition was always reliable: Dorian had known fashion editors and photographers for many years and understood their fads, their methods of work and their phobias, so she was able to direct her 'girls' with a sure sense of the affinity they would have with a future employer. Her methods were pioneering. Finally, after being a budding poet, an engineer in the US Army, a great model, an accomplished mother and the director of the first model agency in France, Dorian was transformed into the perfect hostess. Her brunches, where everyone met, became a regular feature at the start of the season's collections. One of these highly unusual society occasions was even the subject of a special edition of the prestigious television news programme *Cinq Colonnes à la Une!* Once again, Dorian had shown that nothing and no one could resist her.

---

* Dorian was frequently asked to appear on television. She was even the subject of a feature film, with her sister Susy Parker and Eileen Ford, made by Robert Altman for an American TV company. See: Dorian Leigh and Laura Hobe, *The Girl Who Had Everything* (Doubleday, New York, 1980).

Ivy Nicholson

November, 1953. Ivy Nicholson, pale as ivory, with eyes of metallic blue, once more graces the cover of French *Vogue*. The photo is by Henry Clarke, the dress by Balenciaga. The sober elegance of a black fur, with a rose holding the white swansdown collar that completes the outfit: a perfect moment in the history of fifties fashion photography. Ivy Nicholson, now so unjustly forgotten, is one of those legendary models who transformed the cover girl's job into a series of clichés which were never altogether without absurdity: unpunctuality, extravagance, the whims of a star and a chaotic private life. Irresistible one moment, detestable the next, her chief desire was never to leave anyone indifferent towards her. This end always justified the means. She had the colours and delicacy of a tropical butterfly — with a sting!

The daughter of a New York cabbie, Ivy had, at the age of sixteen, grown tired of learning shorthand and left her family and homeland to set out for the Old World with enough to survive for three weeks. Within a fortnight, she was the model most in demand in Paris. With the bearing of an Amazon and the look of Ava Gardner, she was superb. That year —1953 — really was a vintage one for the young woman. In April, Henry Clarke — who understood her beauty better than anyone else — photographed her for French *Vogue* in an off-the-shoulder evening dress by Maggy Rouff, playing with a large fan. It was a fashion photograph that would be as famous as Avedon's 'Dovima and the elephants', two years later. Some models wait in vain, throughout their careers, for an instant like that: the rare, exceptional image that will project them from the ranks of merely delightful, but anonymous faces to the status of a photographic myth — their *Légion d'honneur*, if you will. However, for editors and photographers around the world, working with her could become a torment, and it must surely have been her exceptionally photogenic looks that justified such patience. Ivy would only come to the studio when it suited her, regardless of any agreed timetable. She had no conception of teamwork, or the give-and-take that this necessarily involves. If they wanted her, then they could wait. When she did finally appear (assuming she had decided to do so), Ivy spent an endless amount of time perfecting her make-up, playing with the shadow and light on her face. In her hands, eye-liner and blusher ceased to be mere cosmetics and became paintbrushes contributing to her metamorphosis. She was constantly inventive in this respect, even using white lipstick when the fashion was for throbbing reds. Finally, before leaving her make-up table, she would look at herself one last time in the mirror and, as a ritual gesture, blow a kiss to her own reflection and say: 'Bye-bye, darling, see you soon!'

Above all, Ivy saw posing as playing a part, changing her personality. Chameleon-like, she could become a cat, a china doll or a langorous vamp, as she wished. Her passion for cats had less to do with the serene, poetic affection of Colette, and far more the disturbing, schizophrenic passion of Léonor Fini. Ivy saw cats as the most fascinating of creatures, alternately graceful and bloodthirsty. In front of a camera lens, she could spend hours as a cat, with all her claws showing, recalls Simone d'Aillencourt*, who often had the opportunity to watch her at work. It was not always that simple, however. Quite frequently, when she arrived at the studio, hours late, she would refuse to pose until she had gratified some sudden appetite. If this involved pâté de foie gras, an assistant would be despatched at full speed to Fauchon's. Perhaps she would have an irresistible urge to get out her sketchbook and jot down some vision, so the crew would have to wait a few minutes longer. What else could they do? Unless she got her way, Ivy would lie down in the middle of the studio and refuse to budge. Her entourage would forgive her every one of these whims because she was an irreplaceable asset for the fashion magazines.

Seldom has the career of any model been so intense. Despite her fads and fancies, Ivy Nicholson worked continuously throughout the 1950s, and for most of the following decade — an achievement rare enough for it to be worth mentioning. She was equally able to inspire photographers like Henry Clarke, Erwin Blumenfeld and Guy Arsac, whose preference was above all for haute couture, as well as the new generation, whose offhand manner was so representative of the aesthetic upheavals of the time. For example, William Klein asked her to pose for one of his unusual compositions featured in the October 1959 issue of French *Vogue*; a homage to a Surrealist collage, which was at once a critique and an apology for the consumer society: her face, covered in jewels, emerges beside a wooden hand on the headlights of the latest model sports car — all of Klein in a single shot ! Then there was Guy Bourdin, who for the April 1960 issue of French *Vogue* photographed her in the most exclusive and fashionable clothes, overwhelmed by concrete and metal, at once a foil and a casket for her beauty. At the time, this was a highly provocative way of criticizing the inaccessible luxury represented by these splendid clothes.

Her exotic beauty and demonic charm had immense drawing power. People fought over the unorthodox American. Between a show for Hubert de Givenchy and a publicity campaign for

---

* In conversation with the author in September 1992.

Elizabeth Arden or Peggy Sage cosmetics, Ivy travelled end-lessly, from New York to Verona, to cover the collections. Her life was spent in a succession of rooms, their walls covered with photographs of herself, in luxury hotels around the world — and frequent night-time excursions into the most varied mi-lieux. There was the memorable gala evening at the Théâtre des Champs-Elysées, the high point of the 1960 social season, to celebrate the first complete performance of Tchaikovksy's *Sleep-ing Beauty* in France; the Marquis de Cuevas' last production before he disbanded his company. Ivy, in a black velvet and tulle dress, her own creation, was among the little group of guests who most attracted the attention of photographers: the Maharini of Baroda, Bettina, Princess Fawzia, Anouchka von Mecks and the Begum Aga Khan. On the other hand, she could dance the whole night through on a cabaret table, amid the debris of shattered glasses, having lost all sense of reality, her bare feet covered in blood. On occasion, Ivy would leave home after confiding her newborn baby to one of her precious cats, con-vinced that she had found the perfect babysitter! The next day, she would set off, fresh and bursting with energy, to conquer the fashion pages, never losing any of her constantly teasing charm, an explosive mixture of exhibitionism and narcissism. The great model Jean Dawnay, in her book *Model Girl*, recalls one of Ivy's sensational entrances at the studios of French *Vogue*:

> Ivy Nicholson walked in carrying an enormous painting covered with a cloth, saying it was a painting of herself, and she had brought it to show everybody. We all expected a glamorous portrait of her head, and were somewhat sur-prised when she pulled the cloth off and there, painted in the style of Boticelli, was a life-size nude!

As with so many other great models of her generation, the arrival of the 1960s could very well have plunged Ivy Nicholson into darkness and oblivion. As it was, she found herself more at the centre than ever of international artistic life. After dividing her time between France and Italy, she decided to go into exile in New York, which was then rivalling London for the title of cultural capital of the world. From 1964 onwards Ivy, herself at once a model, a photographer, a poet and a painter, became one of the muses of Andy Warhol, a veritable one-man band in the New York underground scene. The silver-walled Factory, a former industrial space which he transformed into a creative studio from November 1963 to February 1968, became the temple of every kind of experiment. After being the epitome of the luxurious haute couture of the postwar years, the young woman now established herself as one of the most brilliant personalities in this period of rapid change.

When one mentions Andy Warhol, one thinks of him as a painter, which he remained for more than 20 years. But, while never ceasing to paint, he did experiment in other forms of artistic expression: writing, music and, above all, cinema. From a strictly technical point of view, his films begin by rejecting traditional visual and dramatic structures. He worked with a virtually non-existent plot and the final moments of the film brought no change or solution. In fact, all that really mattered was the improvisation of the actors, who were never profession-als. For Warhol, the only point of making movies was to capture on film the extraordinary energy and effervescent eccentricity of those around him. These were true filmed 'happenings'. His favourite subject was human sexuality in all its guises. With a disturbing mixture of incisive humour and complicity, he tack-led the various forms of transgression, which both fascinated and repelled him. Ivy Nicholson appeared in those of his films that most clearly demonstrated this desire to provoke: *Couch* (1964), in which the New York avant garde (Allen Ginsberg and Jack Kerouac appearing alongside Ivy) set out to explore the various sexual possibilities open to a group of adults; *I, a man* (1967), which examined one of the major themes in Warhol's cinema, the life of male prostitutes, in which Ivy 'starred' beside Tom Baker and Ultra Violet. To the public and the media, these works were symbolic of the decadent environment which did so much to create the myth of The Factory.

Warhol's actors were supposed to represent the new cinema idols at a time when the old star system was in decline. All of them tried, through their extravagant behaviour, to awaken the same dreams as the Hollywood stars of the 1930s. A personality like Ivy Nicholson undeniably had that mysterious and intangi-ble screen presence possessed by the former stars of the medium.

Warhol's 'superstars' were soon drawn into the game. The first thing was to choose a strange, unforgettable new name for oneself, to arouse the audience's curiosity. It was a bit like the 'baptism' of a model. In this way, Ivy Nicholson became 'English Ivy', Isabelle Dufresne, 'Ultra Violet', Susan Bottomley, ' International Velvet' and Susan Hoffman, 'Viva.' The men, most of whom were homosexual and transvestites, were not to be left behind. Bob Olivio was transformed into 'Ondine,' Jimmy Slattery into 'Candy Darling', and Paul Johnson became 'Paul America'. The second major stage was to get oneself noticed by every possible and conceivable means. The 'superstars' were haunted by a panic fear of indifference and a frantic desire for recognition at any price. Drugs, incredible clothes and sensational appearances at the most unconventional parties: the quickest way to become famous seemed to be to cause a scandal. The idea was to behave like a temperamental star even before one had really achieved star status. But Ivy's position was more complex because she was already one of the most distinguished models in the world. Warhol took advantage of this, just as he did with Edie Sedgwick.

For Ivy Nicholson, this period was both very exhilirating and infinitely destructive. There was constant pressure at The Factory, which might well have adopted Oscar Wilde's proposition that one owes it to oneself either to be a masterpiece or to wear one. Warhol, who positively worshipped beauty and fame, constantly played host to the latest fashionable models, like Marisa Berenson, Jean Shrimpton, Twiggy, Verushka, Penelope Tree, Benedetta Barzini and Donyale Luna. For Ivy, who was a good deal older, daily life became a constant competition. After wearing the dresses of the greatest Parisian couturiers, and while preserving her legendary elegance, she turned to the considerably more outlandish clothes of stylists like Betsey Johnson, Rudi Gernreich and Joan 'Tiger' Morse, famous for her mini-skirts in aluminum and her electrified ensembles, which everyone wanted to have.

Warhol, often compared to the Sun King in the midst of his courtiers, stimulated conflicts as the fancy took him and according to the interests of the moment. The Factory was the stage for a permanent psychodrama, with everyone trying to catch his attention in every possible way. In this atmosphere of hysteria, Ivy fell madly in love with him, which could only complicate matters: indeed, she even went to the office of *Women's Wear Daily* and announced their engagement! When she was not by his side, she telephoned him at any hour of the day or night to tell him that she was leaving for Mexico, where she would have a quickie divorce so that they could get married as soon as possible. Gradually, confronted by Warhol's continuing indifference, she indulged in more and more frequent scenes. One evening, at the restaurant Max's Kansas City, one of the headquarters of the Counter-Culture, she began to scream and threw a plate in his face. Eventually, Ivy became so aggressive that she was barred from The Factory. As Warhol's relationships with the other inhabitants of his thieves' kitchen were no less passionate, things got worse and worse, until finally they erupted. On June 3, 1968, Valerie Solanas, one of the more unbalanced members of The Factory's outer circle, emptied a revolver at him.

As soon as she heard the news, Ivy rushed to Columbus Hospital on 18th Street, where the artist had been taken. Quite hysterical, she threatened to kill herself at the very moment when Warhol died! It took all the force of persuasion and patience of the actor Louis Waldron to get her to go back home. After a long convalescence, Warhol finally decided to close his doors to anyone even distantly resembling his former entourage. With guards on the entrance, an electronic security system and a barrage of secretaries, it was henceforth impossible to meet him without an appointment. After this change of direction, the lethal madness of the 1960s ended. It meant that Ivy would never be able to realize her dearest wish: to marry Andy Warhol, the most homosexual of homosexuals.

Susy Parker

More than forty years on, her name still irresistibly conjures up
the world of haute couture in the 1950s, when Bettina Ballard
and Carmel Snow were making and unmaking reputations in
the field of fashion. At that time, elegant women throughout
the world were divided between Dior, Fath, Balmain, Chanel
and Balenciaga. It was said in New York that a woman did not
truly know if she was beautiful until she had been judged by
Richard Avedon's Rolleiflex. Susy Parker passed the test bril-
liantly. Her sophisticated beauty, her wit, her incomparable
elegance were such that, despite herself, she became the absolute symbol of the entire period. The word 'glamour' still had
some meaning and it seemed to have been coined for her.

Easter, 1947. Accompanied by her mother, Cecilia Renée
Anne Parker, nicknamed 'Susy', came to join her elder sister

Dorian in New York. The latter had followed in the footsteps of the magnificent Lisa Fonssagrives, at that time the most prestigious model in the world. Dorian had, in her turn, become the favourite face of the great fashion photographers. It was always fascinating for Susy to watch her sister at work, keeping discreetly out of the way. It was at one of these modelling sessions that Irving Penn himself noticed her. Falling instantly under the spell of this red-headed teenager with the green eyes, he suggested that she follow Dorian's example and offered his help in getting her career started. In record time, Susy, then 14 years old, was posing for *Vanity Fair, Vogue* and *Flair*. She started at $15 an hour, the minimum wage for models in the USA. Six months later, she was earning $25 and, after a year, had reached the top of the tree: $60 an hour. Her success was sensational. At the very start of her career, she found herself working in the same week for the four most important magazines in the country: *Life, Look, Vogue* and *Harper's Bazaar*. But Susy had only really wanted one thing since her childhood, and that was to travel. Her dream became reality in February, 1950. She set off for Paris. Invited to pose for the collections under the guidance of her sister Dorian, Susy was at last on her way to Paris, at the age of seventeen. Very soon, in the salons of Jacques Fath, she met the all-powerful Hélène Lazareff and, inevitably, a few days later she was working for *Elle*. These photographs marked the start of a great love affair with the French, but it was not truly consummated until she posed in a Dior wedding dress for the international press. Never was a bride more photographed. Her infallible feeling for a pose, her poise, her slightly cynical sense of humour, together with her sharp, incisive, subtle intelligence and her tendency to make fun of everything, quickly established her in the very masculine world of the photo studios.

However, George Parker, Susy's father, was not happy with this trip to Paris. He wanted her to come straight back home to Texas, on the grounds that while he had given her complete freedom from the age of fourteen, it had been on condition that she stayed in America. Her Parisian success at such a tender age was a constant worry to him and Susy had to return to her family without delay. Once in San Antonio, she decided to continue her modelling career while at the same time going to the other side of the camera and taking up photography. She left for Mexico, hoping to win the $2,500 prize offered by *The American Journal* for the most unusual holiday snap. One day, while she was photographing the house where Trotsky was assassinated in Coyoacan, she met the great reporter Sam Shaw, whose friends Robert Capa and Henri Cartier-Bresson had just founded the Magnum agency. When Shaw happened to show Cartier-Bresson the young woman's photographs of Mexico, Bresson exclaimed: 'I want to see this boy immediately! He's got something! We'll make something of him!'

The 'boy' gladly agreed to become Capa's assistant and to go to Italy with David Seymour, another well-known photographer. She soon had ambitions to become a great reporter, without help from anyone. She set off for the Sahara Desert in search of the unexpected and the unusual. While trying to photograph a leaping gazelle, she fell out of her jeep and twisted her ankle. Legend has it that she was picked up by Legionnaires after she had just shot dead three vultures which were getting ready to pick her bones. In honour of Susy's courage and determination, her new friends offered her a sand lizard, but it did not survive the plane journey from Algiers to Paris.

Capa was killed in Indochina, Seymour during the Suez conflict. For her part, Susy, always between two continents, had attended the 'Carnival at Rio' ball given by Jacques Fath on August 3, 1952, and there met a man of devastating beauty and charm. Pierre de La Salle, test pilot, journalist and prominent member of Vadim's 'gang', was a direct descendent of René Robert Cavelier de La Salle (the explorer who, after travelling around Lakes Ontario, Erie, Huron and Michigan, went down the Mississippi to the Gulf of Mexico). She fell for him instantly and they became inseparable, the playboy and the star model providing material for more than one popular newspaper. Meanwhile, Susy was enjoying huge professional success as one of the first 1950s models to be known and liked by the public at large. With her ideal measurements, she could wear anything. Moreover, for Susy, changing a dress meant changing personality. In this way, she was a sportsgirl in a Jacques Heim, a socialite in a Maggy Rouff, an ingénue in a Givenchy, a dreamer in a Balenciaga and a woman in love in a Dior. Despite that, she was not always easy to photograph. She never kept still and enjoyed making everyone in the studio laugh. Some photographers were captivated by this: Henry Clarke loved to pose her. Susy was one of his favourite models, from the casino in Monte-Carlo to the beach on Barbados. Susy, too, was a great fan of his work. In a recent anthology of Clarke's photographs from the fifties she says: 'I especially remember the photos for the return of Coco Chanel in 1954. He had only half an hour to photograph a pale pink jersey dress in the studio. Just with lighting and by giving me a cigarette holder as an accessory, he turned a simple dress into an event'. The photograph in question appeared in French *Vogue* in March 1954.

The young girl's casual approach, however, could irritate others, such as Horst, who was the first to photograph her for *Vogue* USA, in a dress by Fath, when she was just starting out. Though good friends, they often quarrelled during photo sessions because of Susy's clowning. Avedon, on the other hand, always found it a pleasure to work with her: the young woman's strong personality stimulated his imagination. On one occasion, he photographed her for *Harper's* coming out of the American Hospital at Neuilly, supported by a nurse. Susy, her face concealed behind a vast hat and black glasses, had both wrists bandaged, as if the result of a suicide attempt. The photo, designed to display an Yves Saint Laurent ensemble, caused an uproar.

Susy Parker was so photogenic that the leading cosmetic firms wanted to put her under contract. She was the first great Revlon model and earned $500 a day for studio work with the firm. She also posed for the photographer Holmès Lebel, representing the ideal woman in one of the 'Lux Beauty' campaigns. At the same time as her modelling career, she continued her work as a photographer, both for the Magnum agency and for *Vogue* France, which asked her to take the place of Dick Rutledge, after he had returned to New York. However, what Susy loved most of all was to be with Coco Chanel, whom she had met in 1954, at the re-opening of the salons in the Rue Cambon. Mlle Chanel taught her French — and also taught her that in a photograph, the less you pose, the more 'presence' you have. In the United States, she became the brand image of the famous Chanel No 5, thus putting the seal on a legendary friendship. The clearest evidence of their close relationship? Chanel was the godmother of Susy's daughter, Georgia Belle Florian Coco Chanel.

In 1957, she appeared in 'Think Pink', one of the most successful numbers in the musical film comedy *Funny Face*. At this time, Susy was among the models who were most in demand in the world and taking part in the film was, for her, just an amusing interlude. Shortly afterwards, the same year, while skiing in Klosters, the ultra-fashionable resort immortalized by Deborah Kerr and Peter Viertel, she got a telegram saying: 'Get on a plane for Hollywood. Have part for you opposite Cary Grant.'

Determined to enjoy her holiday, Susy tore up the telegram and even allowed herself the luxury of ignoring a second, equally urgent request. To convince her, the director, Stanley Donen, had to call her in person. Her confidence won, Susy agreed to appear in *Kiss Them for Me*, a comedy about two naval officers on leave, which played on the contrast between the two female stars, both competing for Cary Grant: Susy's elegance was made to offset the good-natured vulgarity of the adorable Jayne Mansfield. When the film opened, *Life* devoted its cover to Susy, on September 23, 1957. Everything was going well for her; so well, in fact, that she decided to devote herself seriously to being an actress. This, however, in no way prevented her from continuing her modelling career. Between advertising campaigns for Revlon and photo sessions for *Harper's Bazaar*, Susy often came back to Paris at the time of the collections and on such occasions would make the covers of all the major periodicals in the country. In this way, the year 1959 is typical, showing the French public's infatuation with the young woman. On February 7, she appeared simultaneously on the covers of *Paris Match* and *Jours de France*, then a fortnight later she was displaying a Chanel dress on the cover of *Elle*. Shortly after that, she appeared twice in succession on the front of *Vogue* (France), firstly in April, for a special number entitled 'Collections-Susy Parker', and then in May.

All the same she was regretfully obliged to leave her sumptuous New York apartment, decorated with African statues, antelopes in precious wood and 14th-century Genoese horses, for the more vulgar luxury of Hollywood. Shortly afterwards, she played Kate Drummond in *Ten North Fredrick*, directed by Philip Dunne from the novel by John O'Hara. Her two co-stars were Gary Cooper and Diane Varsi. The film, with subtlety and tact, describes the relationship between a man and a much younger woman, against a political background. Susy was perfect in the role and the critics were unanimous in praising her intelligent acting. A few months later, she featured in *The Best of Everything*, an adaptation of the novel by Rona Jaffe, directed by Jean Negulesco and starring with Joan Crawford in a role which required her to fall in love with a playwright played by Louis Jourdan. The film, an amusing but trite comedy, contributed nothing to her career or her acting. At the same time she was also invited to play an Andalucian girl opposite Jack Palance as the matador in the television film, *The Death of Manolete*. These were her last carefree days.

The day after filming ended, she received a telegram announcing that her mother was seriously ill, so she took the next plane for San Antonio. Once there, Susy and her father rushed to the hospital, her father driving. Suddenly the road crossed a railroad track. There was nothing to warn drivers if a train was coming, and the signalman had dozed off. Both Susy's arms were broken, and her father, 63 years old, was killed instantly. Shortly after, in hospital, when asked her name, she murmured: 'Mrs Pierre de La Salle.' Only then did it emerge that on August 6, 1955, she had secretly married the handsome young man she had met at Jacques Fath's ball with whom she had so often been photographed. However, their marriage was not destined to end happily ever after. Susy obtained a divorce, and she won custody of their daughter Georgia, then sixteen months old, early in 1961.

She later married the actor Bradford Dillman and retired with him to Santa Barbara. Anxious to break with her past, she devoted herself solely to the upbringing of their children. She became a perfect housewife, even to the extent of baking her own bread. What remained of her years of glory? She carefully kept all her Chanel suits, although she no longer wished to wear them, as a token of her affection for the great 'Mademoiselle'.

Anne Saint-Marie

So far, Anne Saint-Marie is the only great model whose professional and private life have been the subject of a feature film, as opposed to a documentary. In *Puzzle of a Downfall Child*, a director for the first time brutally uncovered the harsh reality of haute couture and fashion photography, whose shooting stars can fall as spectacularly as they rise. In one of the key scenes of the film, the heroine is in hospital, and a doctor asks her: 'You're magnificent. How do you feel?' To which, with humour and despair, she answers: 'Weary of trying to be magnificent.'

Being and appearing superb had become a duty, a constant discipline, as intense as the public eye is pitiless. The whole drama of these women, photographed over and over until they become imprisoned by their enchanting good looks, is in this exchange, with its mixture of irony and genuine dismay. Didn't the North American Indians refuse to be photographed, believing that the camera would steal their souls? A favourite model of Henry Clarke, and an infinitely complex personality, Anne Saint-Marie suffered all her life from the fact that people would only speak of her amazing beauty, without considering the human being or imagining that she could exist in any other manner beneath her impeccable make-up. What remains of her now? A face which, in its perfection, inspires a vague sense of unease while suggesting the wildest of dreams.

Together, Anne Saint-Marie and Henry Clarke created a series of visions; brief, unforgettable apparitions, marked by a grave and often dramatic loveliness — far more than mere fashion photographs intended to show off clothes from the great fashion houses. It was no longer just a matter of a photographer's talent and the 'presence' of the model, of clothes in impeccable taste and carefully selected décors. No mathematical equation could ever explain such alchemy, this sense of osmosis, by which all is at last made transparently clear! What was the great stength of this pair? Clarke managed to photograph her in most of the 'key' dresses of the 1950s, the ones which, more than 40 years later, experts and museums would select as the most expressive of their age: in the September 1953 issues of *Vogue* (France) we are shown, for example, the famous black woollen tunic dress by Balenciaga, the perfect synthesis of the Spanish master's art; a moiré encrusted velvet sheath by Givenchy , which she wore with the same inimitable chic as she did his little shetland dresses with their deceptive simplicity which revealed the couturier's passion for women with an Audrey Hepburn figure; in May 1955, an ermine tailored coat by Balmain, almost a caricature of the 'Jolie Madame' style. . . . These mythical clothes demanded mythical sets.

When Clarke was not working in the studio, he chose places embedded in the collective memory for his backgrounds: the quais along the Seine with their stalls of books, so typical of Paris at that time; the apartments of Mme du Barry in Versailles; the palazzi on the Grand Canal in Venice... Clarke and Saint-Marie always managed to avoid the cliché'd effect of using such backgrounds by only giving them a purely supporting role, never the lead. Only Anne was truly important, representing for the photographer the ideal woman. Never openly seductive or coquettish, distant without being condescending, she did not invite intimacy and yet attracted every eye. Anne's expression hinted at storms to come, an oppressive silence, and the most disturbing mixture of determination and introspection. There was something about her that was at once spellbinding and disturbing. It is hardly surprising that she inspired many imitators among her younger colleagues, all of whom desperately wanted to follow the example of a model who was so different from the norm. We only need to think of the success of the Australian, Jennifer Hockings, in the ambiguous role of her glossy magazine twin. Fascination is by definition a contagious disease. It also struck down the fashion photographers, all of whom — from Jerry Schatzberg to Karen Radkai (and not forgetting Tom Palumbo, whom she married) — wanted at one time or other to work with her.

In 1970, Jerry Schatzberg gave up fashion photography to make his first film, *Puzzle of a Downfall Child*, a tribute to Anne Saint-Marie, who had been his favourite model. The plot: in a house on an isolated beach, a former leading model of the 1950s is recalling her life with a photographer friend, and haphazardly going over her career, her disappointments and her fantasies. As time goes on, there is an increased sense of tragic loneliness, abandonment and deprivation. In 1972, after the film was released in France, Schatzberg explained in an interview with Gérard Langlois for *Les Lettres françaises*:

> The basis of this third script is a tape-recorded interview, lasting three and a half hours, with a famous model whom I knew when I was an assistant photographer. This woman loved to reach out to people, but in return she demanded all their attention. As she never had this profound response, she had to some extent cut herself off from the world, so much so that at the age of 35, having lost contact with reality, she thought she could still do photos where she appeared to be 17 years old. Then she had a nervous breakdown and left to live in an isolated part of Long Island. That's where I went to talk to her. As we were very close friends, she agreed to confide fully in me. Afterwards,

seeing the wealth of material that we had on tape, Carol Eastman, the scriptwriter, and I decided to make a film out of it.

To play Anne Saint-Marie, Schatzberg chose Faye Dunaway, whose sensitive and many-sided interpretation was perfectly suited to the model's kaleidoscopic personality. Talking to the photographer Aaron Rineheart (Schatzberg's screen persona, played by Barry Primus), the heroine tried to reassemble the scattered pieces of the puzzle represented by her chaotic existence: her traumatic adolescence; her début with *Vogue* — at a photo session where the young woman, dressed in veils and feathers, lets herself be upstaged by an irate falcon; her career as a star model — a time of ceaseless anguish as she tries, at all costs, to appear as others wish her to; and, finally, the inevitable lapse into oblivion, which is intrinsic to the job. This can be traced from the appearance of her first rivals (Barbara Carrera, at that time a supermodel, made her acting début as one of them), then the lack of recognition and the indifference which preceded her exile to this house by the Ocean, where her only neighbour is an old Chinese fisherman. . . . One scene, which may be either reality or pure fiction, perfectly sums up the young woman's versatility. She is going to her wedding, dressed in black crepe, like a widow, and escapes before the ceremony, saying: 'Even Garbo refused once.'

The story is all the more disturbing when one recalls that, throughout her years of success, Anne Saint-Marie — or 'Sainte-Marie' as her name was sometimes given in the press — was often compared to the Divine Garbo herself. . . .

As seen by: Hubert de Givenchy

Paris, February 2, 1952. Hubert de Givenchy, twenty-five, is presenting his first collection at No. 8, Rue Alfred-de-Vigny, in the neo-Gothic style mansion, soon to be known throughout the world as 'The Cathedral'. He has asked Bettina, an internationally renowned model who formerly inspired Jacques Fath, to organize the catwalk parade. Serving both as the young couturier's star model and director of public relations (she was the first to set up a press office in the field), the young woman spared no effort, calling on all her friends, the most famous cover girls of the time, to take part. Never in the history of the industry has there been a more prestigious dressing-room!

'Yes, they all paraded for me, each of them with her own personality and charm. Ivy Nicholson was a wonderful model, Sophie Litvak was perhaps more sophisticated, and Susy Parker, in my opinion, was not ideal when it came to presenting a collection but very beautiful in photographs, which was the secret of her success before she became an actress.'

The collection, almost entirely based on contrasts of black and white, was a triumph: apparent simplicity, the appeal of austerity and natural elegance. . . . Clothes, based on the notion of 'separates', which were much easier to wear than those of traditional haute couture, exhibited by the most stunning women of the decade.

'Of course, it was Bettina who probably best symbolized the style of the firm at the outset. She was a most valuable colleague, particularly at the very start, and a superb model, as she had been even before joining me. She stood out from the rest because of her style and expressed a very powerful image of that era.'

Hubert de Givenchy's first collections owe a lot to her personality. He created clothes for her that now belong to the history of fashion: the legendary blouse with puffed sleeves, trimmed in black broderie anglaise, featured in his 1952 Spring-Summer collection and christened after her first name; an evening dress with a cape in white shirting, buttonned from the bottom, above an enormous caramel organza skirt, specially created for Bettina on the occasion of the 'April in Paris' ball, the 1952 version of a famous charity gala on behalf of the French Hospital and the French students' foundation in New York. There was also the centrepiece of the mid-season collections in December that same year, a black silk jersey top, very tightly fitting, with long sleeves, cut straight across the neck, above a pleated satin dress. . . And the back was left totally bare!

Unlike Susy Parker and Ivy Nicholson — 'they just went on the catwalk for me in the early days' — Sophie Litvak was persuaded to work again for the young couturier throughout the year 1952, travelling to Munich and Amsterdam with Bettina in November for the new collection, gala evenings, photo sessions, just like Jacques Fath or Biki. Hubert de Givenchy gave her his most sophisticated models to wear: 'Blond Otter', a 'fur'-printed evening dress; 'Emeralds', a sheath dress in green lace, entirely re-embroidered; 'Rose', a column of black crepe, with a bolero in muslin petals; and 'Imposing', an evening dress in ruby velvet and white satin — to mention only a few of the new models which he entrusted to her in his Autumn-Winter collection, 1952–53. But if one were to choose just one image of her in a Givenchy dress, it would undoubtedly be the photo by Henry Clarke for the February 1953 issue of French *Vogue*, taken in the hammam of the Paris mosque, where she is wearing white lawn trousers embroidered with pineapples, with a bolero in orange cloth and a mauve belt. This portrait, with its exotic charm, recalls Ingres's *Bain turc* or the Moroccan *Odalisques* of Matisse as seen through the lens of Parisian haute couture.

Capucine was also one of Hubert de Givenchy's favourite models from the beginning of 1952. As well as shows for him, she posed for fashion photographs, wearing his finest creations, like the evening dress, in a delicate yellow, with its embroidered top covered by a large shawl in flounced lace featured in his Spring-Summer collection of that year, or one of his inimitable and charming debutante-style dresses in flowered organdie. She was soon a leading figure in his firm, but was at the same time much more to him than merely an elegant trademark. Remembering her, the designer says, with considerable feeling: 'She was, above all, a great personal friend, someone for whom I have a very special affection, and I often think about her.'

They were so close that Capucine called upon him to dress her throughout her life. Years after she had retired from modelling and become a well-known actress, she still showed unfailing confidence in him. Thirty years after their first meeting, no less radiant than ever, she was posing for Victor Skrebneski in a black satin dress, over-printed in gold, which was one of the flagship designs of the Autumn-Winter collection, 1981–82. In the very month of her death, in March 1990, she was photographed by Albert Watson for the Italian edition of *Vogue* wearing a fur and a shantung cape with a white camellia stuck in it — pure Givenchy. Six years earlier, when she was featured on the list of the ten most elegant women in the world, she went to the prize-giving wearing one of his magnificent evening dresses.

Every generation has its own feminine ideal. In the 1950s, the designer worked with all the models who most perfectly crystallized the different aspects of this ideal: Bettina, Sophie, Susy, Ivy and Capucine, but also Denise Sarrault, 'one of my best models and a delightful friend' — China Machado, one of the great Asian beauties of her time, Kouka, the eccentric Argentinian, as well as Jacky, who was picked for her astonishing resemblance to Audrey Hepburn and who went on to have a brilliant career in modelling. Each in her own way contributed to the prestige of the Givenchy name.

In 1956, Hubert de Givenchy and Cristobal Balenciaga took several joint decisions. Firstly, the press was only permitted to see their collections several weeks after the customers and buyers. In addition, the two men refused to allow any photographs to be taken of their creations being worn by anyone except the firm's own models — a minor revolution in fashion journalism! It was also at this point that Givenchy's young women customers, beautiful and refined, began to play an essential role. They were perfect models: on a professional model, a dress always belonged to the realm of fantasy, but on a client it became a part of reality. They would often pose in his very latest outfits for the most prestigious fashion magazines: Dolores Guinness, Fiona Thyssen, Marella Agnelli, Babe Paley — to mention only a few. All were devoted fans. When you ask Hubert de Givenchy to define the part played by his faithful customers and friends, he replies, with his customary tact: 'Their different personalities helped me to assert my own. Of course, the greatest customer associated with the image of the firm was and still is Miss Hepburn'. Audrey Hepburn, who died tragically on January 20, 1993, will always remain the ideal woman for Hubert de Givenchy. A lifelong friend and, for more than forty years, the ambassador of Givenchy elegance throughout the world: this is what Audrey Hepburn represented for the designer. He dressed her on screen and off, creating an immediately identifiable silhouette. Her silky bird-like elegance inspired him to make light, flowing dresses, designs that were apparently very simple but in fact very sophisticated, brushing against the body like a breath of wind: respect for proportions, invisible construction, colour harmony and purity of line. . . . The launch of the scent 'L'interdit' in 1958 subtly indicated the closeness of their association: Hubert de Givenchy created the perfume as though it were forbidden ('interdit') to all other women, and only Audrey Hepburn could wear it; and the star posed for the advertising campaign. The essential elements of their friendship were loyalty, beauty and talent; so much so that in 1985, in the *soirée de l'élégance* at the Opéra Garnier in Paris, a special citation for loyalty went to Audrey Hepburn, who always used to say; 'Monsieur de Givenchy's clothes ward off evil.'

France

Simone d'Aillencourt

Tall, slender and naturally elegant, Simone d'Aillencourt could never go into a clothes shop as a teenager without hearing the same question: 'Are you a model?' So, while on a trip to London to study English, she decided out of sheer curiosity to visit the famous Lucy Clayton Model Agency. The person in charge exclaimed: 'You don't know a thing, but we'll teach you.'

A fortnight later, Simone was on the catwalk in Edinburgh at a prestigious show attended by the most famous designers of the time. She was the unchallenged star of the occasion and, without consulting her, the organizers claimed her to be the new top model at Dior. She was soon working for the greatest London designers, starting with Hardy Amies. The first photos for *Vogue* followed, with the editor, Pat Cunningham, who photographed her in Hyde Park in the rain with two Afghan hounds. All this might seem very glamorous to an outsider, but Simone d'Aillencourt was level-headed enough to admit that there was a lot of work and discipline behind the splendid façade.

At this time, the young woman was constantly making trips backwards and forwards between France and England, which was to be her routine for nearly fifteen years. In Paris, thanks to an introduction from Claude Brouet, she modelled for Cardin in what was to become a long association with him. Like many great photographic models, Simone presented a few collections for Parisian couturiers — which is how she came to work for Jacques Heim while on a trip to South America organized by the Chambre Syndicale de la Haute Couture. As it happens, she was contacted in the early sixties by Yves Saint Laurent and Pierre Bergé who asked her to work exclusively for them. However, she enjoyed travelling, which she did constantly as a model, so she turned down the offer, denying herself the opportunity to show the Saint Laurent collections. In Paris, she also did photos for *Vogue, Elle* and *Jardin des Modes*. These were endless, gruelling days when she might find herself starting a fresh photo session with William Klein which lasted from midnight to five o'clock in the morning, after a working day that had started at dawn with Tom Kublin. Klein refused to work without Simone. Edmonde Charles-Roux commissioned her immediately, turning away the model whom she had originally arranged in order to avoid a diplomatic incident. *Vogue, Harper's Bazaar, L'Officiel* . . . Avedon, Penn, Horst, Blumenfeld, Sieff, Horvat, Clarke, French, Parkinson, Derujinski, Saul Leiter . . . Simone never stopped, particularly as at this time there were very few agencies, so the 'girls' arranged their own schedules and travelled around the world. Simone's few leisure moments were entirely devoted to maintaining some balance in her private life.

One day, Eileen Ford contacted her to come to New York. The invitation coincided with a trip organized by Jansen on the first jet to the USA with the five most beautiful young women in Europe, including Simone. The event attracted a great deal of publicity. Simone spent her time at press conferences, at society events and on television shows. She also met the fascinating, but

quite terrifying Diana Vreeland. It was an historic encounter.
'So, I'm to meet a beauty? Where is this beauty?'
They brought in Simone, who was petrified, and Mrs Vreeland,
without a word to her, took a magnifying glass and examined
her closely before exclaiming: 'This beauty is beautiful!'
An incredible scene, which might have come straight from
Funny Face. But once Diana Vreeland had been won round,
Simone would frequently be signed up during that month.
In 1969, she ended an outstanding career with a photo
session in India for *Vogue* with Henry Clarke. Never had she
been more stunning or more radiant. From 1954 to 1969,
Simone was one of the models most in demand among photographers and editors. Her beauty and professionalism were
certainly enormous assets, but still more was her ability constantly to renew her image. She was able successively to
represent the dressy sophistication of the fifties and the highly
coloured and provocative elegance of the sixties, with disconcerting facility. And yet she still remained herself. Few
models have worked for as long as she did while staying at
the very top. From then on, Simone decided to devote herself to her family. Shortly afterwards, she set up Model
International which, along with Paris Planning, was the greatest model agency in Paris at the time. But, bit by bit, her role
in managing the agency became such that she would have
had to sacrifice her private life for it to continue. She refused and instead founded Image, a more modest agency
which would allow her to live quietly with her husband, the
film-maker José Benazeraf, and their two daughters: Josiane,
the elder, is a lawyer and Béatrice, the younger, works for
the Karin agency. As it happens, Image is much more than a
simple model agency. Simone d'Aillencourt has not forgotten other women as well. To help them to benefit from her
experience in the field of beauty and elegance, she has become an 'image-maker' with a team of professionals to help
her. She offers short courses during which women are helped
to feel more at ease with themselves, taught to make up and
do their hair and given dozens of hints for bringing an element of fantasy into their daily lives. Simone does not forget
that the physical side is nothing without great inner strength,

the source of a genuine contentment; this is why she instructs the many women who come to see her in positive thinking. *Mens sana in corpore sano*: never was Juvenal's maxim so aptly applied.

Bettina

Note: Bettina does not want in any way to talk about her private life, which explains the strictly professional nature of this profile.

On Thursday, November 8, 1990, to mark Photography Month, the Jean-Gabriel Mitterrand gallery paid tribute to the legendary model, Bettina. Guests flocked to admire the photographs taken between 1945 and 1955 by all those who had made fashion into a fully-fledged visual art: Erwin Blumenfeld, Jean Chevalier, Henry Clarke, Richard Dormer, Horst, Willy Maywald and Irving Penn, for a start . . . However, with her inimitable laugh, Bettina refuses to become an 'institution'. Is she nostalgic? Not at all! But, whether she likes it or not, her first name retains its astonishing symbolic power — a key that can miraculously open any lock.

As a girl, Simone Bodin never considered becoming a model. She wanted first to be a painter, then a ballerina (after seeing Janine Charrat in *Swan Lake*) and finally a fashion designer. Jacques Costet, the couturier to whom she showed her sketches when she arrived in Paris, was the first to put a dress on her and to employ her for her spontaneous charm. It was the end of designing clothes. Watching the models at work in Costet's, Simone learned all the essential tricks of the trade — putting on a dress with a scarf over her head so as not to disturb her hair and to stop her make-up getting on the material; making an appearance in the salon, haughty and supercilious, in front of an audience of hand-picked clients; and, above all, withstanding the exhaustion of endless studio sessions — the rudiments of a profession of which she was to become the perfect embodiment. Her professionalism allowed her in just a few weeks to make an impression in fashion shows. Success came with a pink satin déshabillé worn with some black velvet puffed trousers. In parallel with her work as a house model, she also posed for magazines. To start with, she was photographed in the Place de l'Opéra, by the Seeberger brothers — Jules, Louis and Henri — for the weekly *Noir et Blanc*: the pictures were to be the first of many.

After the firm of Costet closed down, a friend sent her to see Lucien Lelong, a dressmaker who was famous for his marriage to Princess Natasha Paley. In a corridor on the day she arrived, she met one of the couturier's assistants, Christian Dior, who told her: 'If Monsieur Lelong doesn't keep you, I'll take you on, because I'm going to open my own fashion house.'

Instantly signed up by Lelong, she missed the opportunity to join Dior and present the famous 'New Look'. Oddly enough, barely a month later, she tired of the Avenue Matignon and went to work for Jacques Fath, the blond, suntanned, eternal adolescent of haute couture. It was Fath who renamed her Bettina and made her famous throughout the world under that single first name.

Bettina was neither inordinately tall nor a femme fatale. She was, however, more accessible than the other models in the house, such as Louise, Tulipe or Paquerette. Fath created a style of timeless simplicity for her which was to be a landmark in the history of dressmaking. On her very first appearance, displaying the Spring-Summer collections in 1948, he got her to show thirty dresses, each more original than the one before. Never had a beginner been more honoured. Before an admiring and well-informed audience, she ended the parade by showing two furs for formal evening wear; one in bronze satin with a bolero trimmed in mink, the other in white satin and mink of the same colour. In a few hours she had become the greatest model in Paris. During the years in which they worked together, Fath was inspired by her personality to design, for her alone, very simple blouses with glossy little white collars, tweed skirts that were very 'Gigi' in style, tweed sailor tops, the first haute couture hunting costumes and evening dresses where the mixtures of colours and patterns were well ahead of their time. To the public, she was so much the epitome of the Fath woman that when the couturier launched his perfume, 'Canasta', in 1950, he chose her to represent the brand image of the scent in the advertising campaign.

After posing for Fath, and for the artists and photographers in the dresses from the very latest collection, Bettina would go, at lunchtime, to the studios of the most prestigious women's magazines to be photographed in clothes by Dior, Grès and Balmain. At three o'clock, she was back in the Avenue Pierre-Ier-de-Serbie for the daily show, only to set out again, later in the afternoon, to work with Jean Marquis or André Ostier. Far from being jealous, Fath actually encouraged her to take on this outside work. As a public relations man, he knew quite well that the more she was in demand, the more her prestige would reflect back on his own fashion house. From time to time, she left him to go abroad. In June, 1949, she went to the USA at the request of the American editor of *Vogue*. Her first session with Penn, in his New York studio, was a veritable nightmare. In the midst of a heatwave, she had to keep the same pose under the lights for five hours on end. Perfection is dearly bought. While she was on one of these working trips to the States, 20th Century Fox offered her an exclusive contract for seven years. She turned it down: it would have meant giving up everything to go and live in exile in California, and she could not contemplate such a sacrifice. In 1952, Bettina agreed to go to London, at the request of her friend John Huston, to do a screen test for the film *Moulin Rouge,* based on the life of the painter, Henri de Toulouse-Lautrec. The idea came to nothing. But her real regret where the cinema is concerned had to do with Luchino Visconti. He was never able to make his screen adaptation of Marcel Proust's *A la recherche du temps perdu.* He was determined to have Bettina for the part of the Princesse de Guermantes. Gradually, the world press began to devote more and more articles to the 'Bettina phenomenon'. When Fath decided to cut her hair very short and transform her into a Greek shepherd, *Paris Match* wrote an article on it, and in no time every fashionable woman wanted to adopt an androgynous look. Cartier-Bresson, doing a rare fashion assignment for *Vogue,* demanded Bettina; and, shortly afterwards, *Life* magazine offered her picture as the portrait of the ideal young Parisienne.

Exhausted by this schedule, Bettina decided to leave Jacques Fath and devote herself exclusively to her work as a model for *Vogue, Harper's Bazaar, L'Album du Figaro,* and also *Elle,* for whom she posed for her first cover, by the photographer Jean Chevalier, in the middle of a profusion of multi-coloured Easter eggs . . . In the early fifties, models in fashion photographs were fixed in dramatic poses and rarely smiled. To achieve this degree of sophistication, Bettina would pay particular attention to her make-up: a very white foundation, darker on the cheekbones, lips outlined with a thin trace of lipliner and eyelids lengthened to enlarge the natural shape of the eye.

At the start of 1952, Bettina was quite happy to go back to the world of the fashion house and went to work for Hubert de Givenchy, who was launching his own creations. As well as becoming his star model, she also took charge of his press service. The 'Bettina' blouse with its puffed shoulders, designed especially for her, went around the world. Such was the young designer's success that he was asked to parade his designs in New York, at the famous charity ball in the Waldorf Astoria, 'April in Paris'. Of course, Bettina was the star of the show. A few days later, they both appeared in the celebrated talk show, *Person to Person,* broadcast by several networks around the country. She had definitely arrived. At the same time, she was also designing collections of pullovers for a Hungarian manufacturer, posing, herself, for the advertising campaigns. Without the slightest doubt, she was an ideal brand image. As time went by, 'Bettina' pullovers were also presented by other great models, such as Marie-Hélène Arnaud, Simone d'Aillencourt, Nico and Carla Marlier.

In 1955, Bettina brought an end to her career in order to enjoy her private life to the full. However, she maintained close links with the fashion world: first, by agreeing to appear on French television in a film about Parisian haute couture, scripted by Françoise Giroud and Frédéric Rossif; and then in 1969, at the request of her friend Gabrielle Chanel, by presenting an entire collection designed for her. Finally, in the early 1970s, she even became fashion director at Ungaro, then head of public relations at Valentino-Paris.

Today, Bettina is a leading figure in Parisian artistic life. She is the 'muse' of Azzedine Alaïa, her closest friend for almost 20 years. She is also a society figure and a model for Pierre et Gilles, whose mixture of refinement and unconventionality delights her. She now devotes herself constantly to the battle against AIDS, just as, from the late 1960s, she worked for ten years to help handicapped children through the French American Volunteers Association (FAVA). It is a kaleidoscopic existence that suits her personality.

Capucine

For connoisseurs throughout the world, Capucine remains the very epitome of the wellbred Frenchwoman, combining distant, sophisticated elegance with, nonetheless, an ever-present glint of humour and self-mockery in her eye: an irresistible mixture. However, while she undeniably belonged to that élite of models who were as much at ease in front of the camera as on the catwalk in a fashion show, she was the only great model of the 1950s, with the possible exception of Susy Parker, who achieved what might properly be called a career in the cinema. Hers was an exemplary professional record.

Born Germaine Lefèvre, in Toulon, she enjoyed an untroubled childhood, thanks to parents who were attentive and affectionate, their whole life revolving around their daughter*: a picture book family. After they moved to Saumur, she carried on with her studies, intending at the time to become a primary school teacher until she suddenly decided on an impulse to give it all up and become a model on the advice of a friend who was a photographer. Having always dreamed of going into the movies, she thought that by posing for magazines or showing clothes, she could earn the money to put herself through drama school. She attended Jacques Charon's class at the Théâtre de l'Oeuvre in Paris while at the same time, after adopting a delicate, poetic new name — Capucine — becoming the darling of Parisian haute couture.

She took part in her first shows for Germaine Lecomte whose house, at that time in the Avenue Matignon, had become famous between the wars for its exceptionally distinguished 'simple little black dresses'. But Capucine was afraid she would suffocate if she were to limit herself to a single fashion house, so she diversified her activities, and worked a lot for advertising campaigns: furs for Andrébrun, Canada Furs and Balmain; jewellery for Sterlé; hats for Albouy, Legroux Soeurs, Maud et Nano, Gilbert Orcel, Paulette and Caroline Reboux. Then, at the start of 1952, after a period with Maggy Rouff, she met Hubert de Givenchy, for whom she was to become a supermodel and a faithful friend. She had a very special liking for the sumptuous evening gowns which he designed especially for her, with evocative names like 'Cristal', from his 1952 Mid-Season collection, a high fashion evening dress in embroidered 'horse-hair' organza and black taffeta, or 'Jaillissante', from his Autumn-Winter collection for 1953-4, a gala dress in tulle. She would always parade with a faraway look and a haughty and impassive air — even though, backstage, she showed marvellous wit, already parodying her own image as an icy beauty to the delight of everyone around her. Between shows, and photo sessions for Givenchy, she travelled frequently at the request of the Chambre Syndicale de la Haute Couture, repesenting Dior as well as Fath or Balmain. Back in Paris, after a session at the

---

* According to some sources, her father was an industrialist, while others say he was a simple employee at the Toulon arsenal.

studio, she worked for the most famous fashion photographers, from Henry Clarke with whom she did her first cover in 1954 for the July/August issue of French *Vogue*, to Sam Levin, via Guy Arsac, Jean Chevalier, Robert Randall, Sante Forlano and Sabine Weiss.

But the young woman whom her friends called 'Cap', never lost sight of her original objective, which was to act. She had a small part in Jacques Becker's 1949 film, *Rendez-vous de Juillet*. It was on the set of this film that she met and married the actor Pierre Trabaud, though the marriage lasted only six months. Then, in 1958, she left France to settle in New York. The story goes that John Wayne was dumbstruck when he saw her in a fashionable Manhattan restaurant. He invited her to Holly-wood to test for his next film, *Rio Bravo*. Unfortunately, Capucine's English was not quite good enough for the role, which eventually went to Angie Dickinson. In the event, it was the agent Charles Feldman who really started her on her career in the cinema. Thanks to him, she appeared first of all in *Song Without End* (1960), a film begun by King Vidor and finished by George Cukor. Her two main partners were Dirk Bogarde, who played Franz Liszt, and Geneviève Page, another aristocrat of the French cinema, playing Countess Marie d'Agoult. Capucine, dressed by the talented Jean-Louis and photographed by James Wong Howe, was more lovely than ever as Carolyn, Princess of Sayn-Wittgenstein, even though some people criticized her for not expressing a great deal of emotion. The film, which showed Liszt torn between music, religion and women, was a pure Hollywood melodrama. At the time, people spoke of a romance between Dirk Bogarde and Capucine. She even went to join him in his house at Little Chalfont, Amersham, in the heart of Buckinghamshire, and lived there for some time. The inter-national press, always keen to get a personal story, besieged the couple in the hope of uncovering more details. But Capucine showed herself to be inflexible where her private life was concerned and always refused to give way to the temptation to reveal anything. However it may be, there was a deep and enduring friendship between the two actors. The same year, she finally made a film with John Wayne, Henry Hathaway's *North to Alaska*. Who would have thought it? Capucine in a Western. The film was a success at the box office and the start of a great love affair with the Americans, which — regretfully — she never had with the French.

In 1961, she appeared in *The Triumph of Michael Strogoff*, directed by Victor Tourjansky, in which she appeared opposite Curt Jurgens as Tatiana, a spy in the stereotypical mould of a 'Mata Hari'. The Steppes of Central Asia in Technicolor, gipsy violins and thwarted love . . . in short, a huge dose of kitsch. A year later she met William Holden on the set of Jack Cardiff's *The Lion*. It was the start of a passionate affair between two apparently quite opposite characters: Capucine was haughty and refined, Holden, rough, alcoholic and attracted to taking every sort of risk. But the meeting of opposites is often the recipe for a successful chemistry: Marlene Dietrich and Jean Gabin are another perfect example. The affair caused a scandal because Holden was married. He was the last man officially to be mentioned in Capucine's life; she was even called 'the most confirmed celibate in cinema.' A few months after her affair with Holden, she appeared in the cast of Edward Dmytryk's *Walk on the Wild Side*, with Jane Fonda and Barbara Stanwyck. This outstanding trio of women did not enjoy the success one might have expected. But, as far as Capucine was concerned, she would not be discouraged. What actress, however talented, has not had at least one box-office failure?

Then, in 1963, she was in Blake Edwards' *The Pink Panther*, with Peter Sellers. Her intepretation of Inspector Clouseau's wife was an accomplished masterpiece of humour. Capucine was not only a stunning beauty, but a fully-fledged actress. Other directors also allowed her to bring subtlety and flavour to her roles. First there was Clive Donner, in 1965, with *What's New Pussycat?*, where, playing alongside Peter O'Toole, Romy Schneider, Peter Sellers and Ursula Andress, in a script by Woody Allen, she was irresistibly funny as a nymphomaniac society woman. But the high point of her acting career was undoubtedly the part of Princess Dominique in Joseph L. Mankiewicz's *The Honey Pot* (1967). Opposite Rex Harrison, Maggie Smith and Susan Hayward, Capucine honed to perfection — with a nice sense of caricature — her role as an aristocratic lady prepared to do anything to achieve her ends. Even though, in

1969, she made *Satyricon* with Fellini, a director of genius, she would never truly recapture the quality of her previous roles. She was still to be seen in films of variable quality, like *Fräulein Doktor*, *Moeurs cachées de la bourgeoisie*, *Soleil rouge* and *Balles perdues*; and on television in *Madame et ses flics*, *La Griffe du destin*, *L'Amour du risque* and *Détective gentleman*, which was her last performance, in the late 1980s. In all these parts, she was always incomparably beautiful, even though the scripts had little to recommend them.

Her life ended in deep solitude. Her fans could still see her at the European cinema awards ceremony, reading out a letter from Federico Fellini, or on the cover of Italian *Vogue*, in the month of her death, looking more magnificent than ever. Only a few faithful friends, among them Audrey Hepburn and Hubert de Givenchy, managed to meet her face-to-face. For nearly 20 years she had lived alone in Lausanne, Switzerland, with her three cats. After devoting a lot of time and energy to helping the victims of the conflict in Lebanon, she was unable to bear the news that she was seriously ill. Some time during the night of Saturday 17 to Sunday 18 March, 1990, Capucine leapt into the void from her eighth-floor apartment.

Sophie (Litvak)

At the start of the 1950s, the foreign press was inclined to remark that Sophie was as Parisian as the Place Vendôme, and just as famous. It was a cliché, of course, but there was some truth in it for all that. She was chiefly someone who embodied a state of mind, a sensibility. Although far from being a flawless beauty, she still became the archetype of France in the postwar period: elegant, witty and playful. She was not dreamy like Bettina, or enigmatic and mysterious like Capucine and Denise Serrault, nor did she have the aristocratic and slightly condescending bearing of Simone d'Aillencourt. She did, however, occupy a place in the world of French cover girls at that time which was entirely her own. In her case, it was less a case of perfect features and an ideal figure than a personality, unique of its type, which crystallized all the hopes of a country in the midst of reconstruction, thirsty for freedom and escape from worries; in short, a sign of good health.

Simone Steur (her real name) made her début as a model with Hermès, whose dress and accessories departments had been famous throughout the world since the twenties, thanks to designers such as Lola Prusac. Her chief assets were a radiant smile, high cheekbones, silky auburn hair with reddish highlights, a wasp waist and a very attractive vivacity in her movements. Such was her charm that Lucette Hervieu, the house designer, did not hesitate for an instant to take her on and start her modelling swimsuits, despite Sophie's peculiar figure: her excessively long upper body and rather short legs were handicaps which she had to circumvent throughout her life. Bit by bit, she also modelled leather clothes (the firm's speciality), dress suits and printed silk cocktail dresses. From then on, as graceful on a catwalk as in photographs, she was able to double her income by posing for fashion magazines. Everybody who was anybody, from the Duchess of Windsor to Bébé Bérard, attended the Hermès shows — and that included the major Parisian dressmakers, such as Jacques Fath, who came as friends. As soon as Fath saw Simone, he clamoured to have 'that little model at Hermès who is becoming the queen of their *cabine**.'

When she joined Fath, at the very start of 1949, she was twenty-three years old and still called Simone. Rechristened Sophie by the young dressmaker Pygmalion, she soon established herself as one of the most famous models in the capital and was much in demand as a photo model. Lucky, one of the stars of Dior who had started with Sophie at Hermès, said in 1961, it was 'her self-confidence, her determination and her desire to make it,' plus the dazzling sense of life and youth that she conveyed, that explain her overnight success. The year 1949 was truly a crucial one for Jacques Fath, marked by three important events: on May 27, Rita Hayworth married Prince Ali Khan in a Fath dress, thus bolstering his prestige throughout the world; Louise, one of his favourite models, whose inimitable style was to inspire generations of her fellow-models, left him

---

* Freddy, *Dans les coulisses de la haute couture parisienne* (as told to Jean Carlier), Flammarion, Paris, 1956, p. 37.

for good; and, finally, Sophie joined his group of house models, in a sense taking over from Louise in the role of sophisticated 'muse' of the firm.

The couturier did not only change her first name, he decided to remodel his new protégée entirely. With the help of the hairdresser Georgel, he had her hair cut, thus giving more character to her face. Then, slightly provocatively but with a great deal of humour, he set out to exploit the contrast between her feminine body, which was very slender and ideal for low-cut evening dresses, and her unexpected air of a young page boy. From her very first show, for the Spring-Summer collections of 1949, Sophie was made responsible for sharing the most significant designs in the new styles with Bettina. She scored a real triumph with 'Bulle d'eau', an evening dress made from sixty metres of grey-green tulle, topped by a cape and beret set all over with sparkling sequins matching the bustier. This dress, which had taken three workers a month to make, was ordered by Maria Montez for the film *Portrait d'un assassin*. Fath, an inspired colourist, juggled with the most delicate tints and, throughout his association with Sophie, made her wear the most refined combinations of colours and materials: for example, a gala sheath in moss green velevet, its décolleté decked with a mass of 'parma violet' ribbons for the Autumn-Winter collection 1949-50; or the evening dress in pleated tulle, shading from orange to yellow, through mandarin and fresh mango, aptly named 'Sunbeam' for Spring-Summer 1951. Sophie cooperated in all his whims: a wide-brimmed, 'ducktail' hat, a shagreen satin sheath, and the first haute couture 'Western' outfits!

The whole of Fath's salon, with the exception of Bettina, had a particular reputation for its sarcastic and biting wit. Berthe, the irascible *chef de cabine* in charge of the models, was often the target of cutting remarks as were many other figures in the fashion world: well-known models, famous customers or great designers. Sophie, who had a constantly sparkling sense of humour, was much more than a supermodel. Popular both for her elegance and for her delightful conversation, she was very soon a regular frequenter both of Parisian salons and Jacques Fath's unforgettable parties. Among these we may mention the Square Dance Ball which he gave on August 6, 1950, at his house in Corbeville. Reflecting its theme of the American West, Sophie appeared on the arm of Stanley Marcus of the famous Dallas store. She was also quickly picked up by the cinema (she appeared in the film *Modèles de Paris* when she first arrived at Fath's) and the fashion magazines — *Vogue, Elle, L'Officiel de la Couture et de la Mode de Paris, Jardin des Modes, La Femme Chic, Noir et Blanc* and *L'Album de Figaro*, as well as the foreign press. At the request of the most prestigious photographers of the time, from Henry Clarke to Clifford Coffin, via Cecil Beaton and Horst P. Horst, Sophie posed in clothes by Rochas, Balmain and Rouff. A remarkable record.

When Sophie joined Jacques Fath, Bettina had been the accepted star model for more than a year. Instead of feeling the slightest jealousy towards one another, they soon became friends, despite the desperate efforts of the press, which is always in pursuit of signs of rivalry between two muses of the same artist. As Praline recalls in her 1951 memoirs, *Praline, Mannequin de Paris,* 'Fath's salon, in the Avenue Pierre Ier de Serbie, is one of the summits of Parisian elegance; Sophie and Bettina are its most remarkable inhabitants, their beauty and charm contrasting and complementing one another.' In fact, the designer always made an effort to bring out the contrast between them, which was evident both on the catwalk and in front of the camera. At a press show, Sophie would tend to show the most elegant numbers, while Bettina took the more girlish dresses which she wore with the charm of an adolescent. In her photographs, Sophie was always supremely poised, regardless of the film's speed, lighting or pose, while Bettina was so changeable that she managed to transform herself in every shot, making her invaluable for fashion editors. Indeed, the two women had known each other even before they arrived at Fath's: their first meeting was in the spring of 1946, in Nice, when they frequented the same group of friends, with Christian Marquand and Pierre de La Salle as its leading members. Once they became famous, they grew closer and closer to one another, loving to work together, both in France and abroad. Thus, in June 1949, Bettina made her first trip to the United States to work with Irving Penn and was met on her arrival in New York by Sophie, who was the darling of the American magazines and living in an elegant Park Avenue apartment for a few weeks before joining Jacques Fath. When not on some professional assignment, they would meet and go out a lot together, with such friends as the black photographer Gordon Parks, one of the most daring cameramen for *Life* magazine, whom they publicly defended against racist attacks, and Philippe de Croisset, who was among the most cosmopolitan Frenchmen of his generation. One day, Croisset invited our two ambassadors of Parisian style to spend a weekend in a 'country club'. For Sophie and Bettina, who thought they would at last be able to relax among friends, this seemed an ideal outing, so they set out in linen slacks and cotton blouses, without a single evening dress — only to find that it was one of the most select clubs in the region, where everyone changed clothes at least three times a day. The management was outraged and forced them to have dinner between two screens and to use the service staircase. They could hardly stop giggling! However, their most striking memory was in 1951, when they were both in Brazil to exhibit the very latest Dior collection with Alla and Sylvie, the two Dior star models. Sophie and Bettina, always on the lookout for excitement, dared each other to take part in an exorcism ritual organized by some cult or other. They recalled the smell of ether, the throbbing chants, the priests in a trance and hysterical outbursts from several of those taking part. Ten years later, Bettina was amused to think that they had been so completely casual about it, going there without the least protection!

Sophie's fame was such that many couturiers would inevitably call on her for a press show or a gala. Of course, these included Hubert de Givenchy, as well as Biki, the eccentric Italian designer. Grand-daughter of the composer Puccini, she had made a name as an innovator in 1937, by suggesting unexpected colour combinations. Later, in the 1950s, her work combined the imagination of Fath and the delicacy of Balmain with the daring of Schiaparelli. For her shows, she would leave her firm's headquarters in Milan and go to the most prestigious locations in Italy. The 'première' usually took place in the evening, at the Venice Lido, attended by the whole of 'Café society'. In this way, Sophie, who was a great admirer of Biki's designs, showed them off to Ingrid Bergman, Valentina Cortese, the Duchess Visconti and Alida Valli, all customers of the house and friends. At the end of the show, the models posed for the press on gondolas along the Grand Canal, wearing the most spectacular dresses.

The end of Sophie's modelling career did not in any way mean retirement and neglect. Instead, on December 2, 1955, she married the great Russian director Anatole Litvak, 24 years her senior. Both had been married before: Sophie to François Malgat, a leading figure in society in Nice, and 'Tola' (as he was called) to the Hollywood star Myriam Hopkins. Sophie would accompany her husband around the world on location and took up journalism, writing for *Fémina* and *Elle*. They made a brilliant and famous couple, much in demand. Their 'Sundays' were a meeting-point for the cultural, political and social élite of the day. There were lunches at Louveciennes with the Lazareffs, dinners which Guy Schoeller had organized for the Pompidous, and meanwhile they would go to Klosters to meet their many friends, such as Irvin Shaw, Peter Viertel, Deborah Kerr and Noel Harrison, or go down to Sardinia with the producer Sam Spiegel. Whenever they were depressed, Sophie — nicknamed 'Aunt Sophie' by her close friends — would take them for a cruise on Sam Spiegel's yacht to revive their taste for living. Friendship, more than anything else, played a central role in her life. Her two closest companions were Françoise Sagan and Jacques Chazot. These happy years ended on December 16, 1974, with Anatole Litvak's death. Sophie never got over it and shortly afterwards succumbed to cancer and a stroke. A few days later, the Drouot auction rooms sold off her effects: several decades of elegance, emotions, laughter and tears . . . a whole universe.

Denise Sarrault

'I was born in the year of three queens: Elizabeth II in Great Britain, Marilyn Monroe in the United States and Denise Sarrault in France — in Paris, of course!' The tone is one of merriment, of clear, happy laughter, very different from the sphinx-like image she presented, of an enigmatic and infinitely remote beauty, dressed in a man's trench coat — 'my second skin' — the subject of a film on the cult television programme *Dim Dam Dom* with the apt title, 'Beyond a Face'*. From 1948 to 1968, Denise Sarrault was a great model for Hubert de Givenchy, Pierre Cardin and Valentino, and an unforgettable model in the viewfinders of such photographers as Jeanloup Sieff, Helmut Newton and Tom Kublin. By turns a flower woman, an appari-

---

* *Au-dela d'un visage*, also known as *Un mannequin et après*.

tion in the style of Joseph von Sternberg or an intangible and fragile wanderer, bearing the scent of tuberose, she drifted through many imaginary worlds, leaving in her wake a distaste for the commonplace and a host of regrets: a rare presence indeed.

Denise Sarrault began as an assistant to Henriette Boudreau, whose little dress house had become famous for making wedding dresses for the aristocracy of the Faubourg Saint-Germain. When the designer moved to the Rue Royale, Denise naturally followed her. But here, a few yards from Lalique, her career took a new turn. One of the best connected salesgirls, the daughter of the actor Louis Jouvet, was so insistent that Denise finally presented herself, on her recommendation, at Lanvin. Countess Marie-Blanche de Polignac, 'fragile and delicate to the point of instability' and the daughter of Jeanne Lanvin herself (who had died two years earlier), saw her and exclaimed: 'She has very pretty shoulders!' On the strength of that alone, Denise was instantly hired.

Her arrival at Lanvin's coincided with a major trip that the house was about to undertake across Morocco. Of course, since Denise was still new, she couldn't go along. The rules among the house models are very strict: every 'girl' has to serve her apprenticeship before taking part in an event of that sort. One of the Lanvin models, Maryse Kramer, the daughter of a rich Egyptian family and a Silvana Mangano lookalike, at once took care of Denise, this strange and timid creature who seemed so utterly lost that the *chef de cabine* had unkindly christened her 'Nestling'. Under Maryse's wing, she was gradually able to surmount the petty rivalries that are an inevitable feature of the closed world of haute couture. Meanwhile, Dominique, one of the star models, had to pull out of the Moroccan trip because she had just met Jean Gabin who was begging her to stay behind and marry him as soon as possible. With Maryse's help, Denise was able to replace her; so, only a few days after her debut in the fashion world, she was travelling around Morocco, staying at the legendary Mamounia and taking part in lavish festivities in the mountains, which the Glaoua had organized in their honour. The trip really took on an extra significance because, on their return to Paris, Denise, between showing Lanvin's dresses, undertook several tours on behalf of the Chambre Syndicale de la Haute Couture, the industry's Chamber of Commerce: to Australia; to South Africa, where she was accompanied by Praline and represented Madame Grès and Christian Dior; to Mexico, where she did her first advertising campaign for the famous Del Prado hotel group, photographed in a swimming pool covered in white gardenias; and to the United States, which she was able to visit thanks to a member of the Marshall Plan in Rome and his wife who had taken a liking to her when she saw her modelling in Monte Carlo. Denise loved all this travelling around the world on trips that might last up to three months and which always took place in a very civilized and very happy atmosphere. Remember: in 1948, it took four days to reach Australia! There would be stopovers in London, Cairo, Colombo and Singapore. The travellers did not fly at night, so they could take advantage of a restful sleep in the local luxury hotels. Denise never tired of travel, whatever the destination, but hated to stay in Paris. Unattached, always between one flight and the next, she decided to take a permanent room in the Hôtel de la Trémoille, 'my private hotel in Paris', the aristocratic charm of which delighted her. She went there in 1950 and was to stay 20 years: it served her as family home, refuge and salon, for every sort of party, where you might bump into Nureyev, Lena Horne, Gene Kelly or Verushka, brought there by Denise, not forgetting the entire Argentinian polo team.

In 1955, Denise was invited to attend a Givenchy show by her friend Colette, one of the house models. At the last moment one of the 'girls' fell ill and, Denise, purely and simply, agreed to take her place. Shortly afterwards, Hubert de Givenchy signed her on permanently to replace Joan, a splendid American who was leaving him to marry Count Moncada. Her arrival in the Rue Alfred de Vigny coincided with the 'Sabrina' style. Billy Wilder's film of that name, first shown in Paris on February 4, 1955, was a huge success and gained universal admiration for the irresistible elegance of Audrey Hepburn combined with Hubert de Givenchy. In fact, Denise modelled the famous black and white evening dress that the star wears when she dances with William Holden. Even now, she still nostalgically recalls the very affectionate professional relations that existed at the fashion house in the Parc Monceau. Every day was marked by an atmosphere of absolute elegance and courtesy, and a genuine 'family spirit' existed between the couturier and his fellow-workers. Indeed, the young model never had the feeling that she was going to work at all. She was always fascinated by Hubert de Givenchy, because as soon as he designed a dress, one could always tell which model would wear it. The young designer, who perfectly understood her extravagant personality, liked her to show his most eccentric creations: his rose and green-tinted furs; his evening hats, which were very spectacular, oval or spiralling and tipped back (Autumn-Winter collection 1955-56); his cocktail dresses with balloon skirts hung with hoops of scarves (Autumn-Winter collection, 1957-58); the first wigs, in unusual colours, but natural hair, made by the Carita sisters (Spring-Summer collection, 1958); and short chiffon caftans, split to reveal a sheath (Autumn-Winter collection, 1958-59) — to mention only a few.

Thanks to Hubert de Givenchy, Denise had the immense good fortune to meet Cristobal Balenciaga. At this time, the Spanish designer would regularly come to comment on his young disciple's collections and the models were delighted to perform for them alone. One day, Balenciaga invited them into his house in Madrid to organize the Givenchy show at the same time as his own. At the end, he offered a dress to each of the models: 'Choose whichever one you like . . .'

Denise had no hesitation in choosing for herself a very simple dress in black jersey, in the famous 'sack' style, which she had modelled under a sable coat. She wore it for years before losing it on one of her many journeys. Another wonderful memory: she met Fred Astaire, through Audrey Hepburn, during the making of *Funny Face*. The famous dancer invited her to dinner and when he came to fetch her from the Hôtel de la Trémoille, the doorman almost fainted on seeing his favourite star. After dining at the Berkeley, they danced all night at Fred's in the Rue de Ponthieu, to a Latin-American band.

Throughout this time, Denise was often away on trips: for Givenchy, of course, but also for other major houses at the request of the Chamber of Commerce. At the same time, she often posed for fashion magazines, working with Henry Clarke

— for whom she did her first pictures for *Vogue* France in October 1955 — Richard Dormer, Sante Forlano, Donald Silverstein, Jerry Schatzberg, Philippe Pottier and Alec Murray (who always worked as a team with the illustrator Nino Caprioglio). She never gave up the search for new experiences and in 1959 decided to leave Hubert de Givenchy, dividing her time between photo sessions and press shows for her designer friends. In this way, she showed Valentino's first collection in Rome, stepped onto the catwalk with Hiroko Matsumoto and Simone d'Aillencourt for Pierre Cardin, was the star of the first Bohan collection at Dior's and became a famous regular at Roberto Capucci's shows at the Pitti Palace in Florence.

Denise Sarrault has no doubt that Jeanloup Sieff — 'my good-luck charm' — started her 'real' modelling career. In eight legendary photos, taken in Monte Carlo and published in April 1960 in *Le Jardin des Modes*, she finally became an outstanding model. Sieff managed to reveal her beauty, halfway between Greta Garbo and Marlene Dietrich, in all its subtle and disturbing ambiguity. A very pale, emaciated face, like a star of silent cinema, hollow eyes, a piercing look and a faint, ironic smile. The personality was the opposite of that demanded by normal commercial considerations. How could a reader and potential customer identify with such an image? However, these peculiarities, far from setting her apart, would become her strength. The photos with Sieff, which are clearly the product of a chemistry between them, aroused such keen interest that they would subsequently often work together: for *Le Jardin des Modes*, naturally, where Denise was to appear on the cover of the May issue that year as well as in a Sieff photo shoot set in Morocco, but also for *Harper's Bazaar*, where he photographed her in evening dresses on the sets of the film *Cleopatra.*

Helmut Newton also played a major role in Denise's career, and she was his first great model. In the summer of 1961, she had the opportunity to work with him for the June-July edition of French *Vogue*, which had finally commissioned him. He had been fascinated by Denise, even when he was still living in Melbourne. He shot her in a very Mata Hari style, but with his own inimitable signature, in a selection of luxurious furs, at the Ritz and at the Cartier boutique. A month later, they were doing their first report on the latest fashion collections for the September issue. And when in the spring of 1962, Denise was invited by Oscar Orstein to organize a trip to Rio de Janeiro to promote the designs of the young Gérard Pipart, at this time a designer for the firms of Bellerive, Sport-Plage and Stanley on the Côte d'Azur, Newton covered the event, again at the request of French *Vogue* for their May issue. There were scenes of getting out of the plane, exterior shots and parades at the Copacabana Palace. The trip was important in several ways. Until then, Brazil (and South America as a whole) only knew about Parisian haute couture, and Denise Sarrault was the person who introduced French ready-to-wear clothes to the country at the height of the carnival season. For Newton, Denise was 'the archetype of the French girl, sublime, cold, tall, mysterious, beautiful, with a hollow face and broad shoulders'. He loved photographing her so much that years later he was to say that throughout the whole of the 1960s, his three favourite models had been — in that order — Denise Serrault, Mercedes and Wille Van Rooy.

At this time, Denise posed for the most refined practitioners of photography as an art form: Duane Michals, Bob Richardson, Francesco Scavullo, Elizabeth Novick, James Moore, Ica Vilander, Diana Arbus — and Sarah Moon, who took her first fashion photographs, on the far side of the camera, with Denise at the Gare de Lyon in 1960. What might sound like a tiresome list, a Who's Who of fashion photography in its most tumultuous decade, is in fact highly revealing in terms of the aesthetic preferences and affinities it suggests. Denise Sarrault always sought out the most individual and unusual image-makers.

It was on a journey to Italy with the photographer Hugo Mulas that Denise discovered Verushka who, before becoming a model, studied painting in Florence. Since she herself had been encouraged throughout her own professional career by women capable of discerning her genuine originality, she now, in turn, supported the young German aristocrat, just as she had the models China Machado and Kouka when she was with Givenchy. Mysterious links, she knew, join the past to the present. No one can now doubt the significance of the encounter: Denise's succession was assured.

In 1968, she gave up modelling, but without abandoning the world of fashion where she had many friends, such as Peggy Roche and Tan Giudicelli. For nearly five years she was to be one of the most prized editors of the weekly *Elle*: her practised eye and unique taste made her an exceptional contributor. Then, in 1973, she left the world of women's magazine publishing and spent the next six years organizing shows for the Chamber of Commerce and the Fédération Française du Vêtement. Meanwhile, marriage to Jean-Paul Najar, a collector of contemporary art, brought her still closer to the leading circles in haute couture. In 1985, in homage to his wife, he began to show a series of collections of dresses and hats, called 'Moody Hats', which were genuine sculptures, witty and provocative, that one could interpret according to one's mood. Some examples, each unique, were even donated by the elegant Madame Hearst to the Brooklyn Museum, in New York. In 1990, Denise posed for the Catalan photographer Tony Bernard in some of Jean-Paul Najar's creations. The pictures were published in the magazine *Up and Down*.

At the end of the 1980s, Denise, always a wanderer, opted for the sunny, sensual charm of Barcelona which she preferred above anywhere else in the world. The city is both an international port and a cultural melting pot; she loved it so much that in January 1991 she agreed to organize a prestigious exhibition of her best photographs in one of the city's galleries.

On the occasion of the exhibition at the Gallery Capital A, in the Paseo de Gracia, the Spanish television channel, Canal +, made a film entitled: 'La Belle Denise'. Not long afterwards, a flood destroyed a trunk containing four genuine Chanel suits, from the 'Mademoiselle' period, and a Givenchy ribbon bolero, which she had carefully preserved: her haute couture souvenirs had been reduced to nothing in a matter of seconds. The trunk, christened with a mournful touch of humour 'Mourir à Barcelone' ('Death in Barcelona'), was for some days the main attraction in the town. Society folk, intellectuals, young dandies and onlookers of every kind came past to pay homage to this vestige of times past.

Great Britain

Fiona Campbell-Walter

The 1950s saw the high point in the history of sophisticated and elegant models who embodied an ideal vision of the woman of the world for the photographers and dressmakers. For some of these women, the job was merely that: at the end of the day, they said goodbye to sable, high fashion and rivers of diamonds. They left the studios and hurried back to husbands and children in a cosy, welcoming refuge from high society and its ways. But there were others whose personal lives coincided with the role of aristocratic beauty that they were asked to play for the glossy magazines. This was the case with Fiona Campbell-Walter. The favourite model of Cecil Beaton (the most 'Proustian' of fashion photographers), she enjoyed an exceptional career. She came from an upper-class family, was always wonderfully turned out, whatever the occasion, and made headlines in the gossip columns. The coincidence of image and reality contributed to Fiona's success. The public saw her as the true-life heroine of a romantic novel, promising the realization of every kind of dream.

Fiona had been driven by an ambitious mother who was well aware of her daughter's potential and, while still a teenager, found herself in front of the cameras of Henry Clarke, whom she had met in London. He was immediately struck by her incredible photogeneity, combined with an inborn dress sense, an understanding of how to pose and exceptionally delicate gestures. She had every quality needed to reach the top in modelling. She joined the Lucie Clayton agency and quickly became a star of many editions of *Vogue*. She was so successful that she had the rare privilege, even for a famous cover girl, of appearing on the cover of *Life* magazine on January 12, 1953.

She knew all the little tricks needed to perfect her look. For example, she would lighten her splendid red hair at the temples, in order to give greater depth to her eyes, an effect that was especially successful in photographs. Her hair was long enough for her to adopt any style. She never sacrificed it to the whims of fashion, so she was able to remain herself, and at the same time to stir the imagination of fashion editors and photographers, from John French to Horst, via Norman Parkinson, Gene Fenn, Sabine Weiss, Frances McLaughlin, Richard Dormer, Sante Forlano and Robert Doisneau, to mention only a few. Henry Clarke frequently worked with his protégée and had a sure instinct for the best way to bring out her natural elegance, whether she was wearing a Schiaparelli evening gown or a swimsuit on a Sicilian beach. But it is Cecil Beaton who remains the most celebrated of her admirers. His work had started to appear in *Vogue* in 1924 and he was equally talented as a photographer, illustrator, columnist and creator of costumes for stage and screen. A well-known figure in society, he was naturally attracted to Fiona, since she was a direct descendent of the prestigious Campbells, one of the leading Scottish clans. For Beaton, who was an admirer of the British Royal Family — and its official photographer — this ancestry, combined with quite remarkable personal qualities, was irresistible.

In 1956, Fiona married Baron Hans Heinrich Thyssen. The

handsome art collector, born in the Netherlands in 1922, was the heir to one of the largest steel manufacturers in the German Federal Republic. He and Fiona seemed an ideal couple; an alliance of culture and beauty with power and glory. The wedding took place on September 18 in Castagnola, near Lugano. Fiona looked radiant on the arm of her father, a rear admiral in the Royal Navy. She was wearing a gift from the bridegroom, a superb pearl necklace valued at thirty-five million francs, a fact which was mentioned repeatedly by the international press, who were gathered to report the event. She became the third Baroness Thyssen, after Princess Teresa de Lippe and the great Anglo-Indian model, Nina Dyer. Shortly after the honeymoon in Sicily, they settled at the Villa Favorita, one of Thyssen's many homes, which had been acquired by his father in 1937. Hans Heinrich installed himself there ten years later. The Villa Favorita was made up of several houses and gardens, as well as a museum to house the huge family art collection, and was a frequent venue for carefully selected parties of the 'Beautiful People'. When the Thyssens were not in Lugano, they stayed in Jamaica or Saint Moritz. They frequented the famous Palace Hotel where, under the aegis of Caprice Badrutt and her husband Andrea, the Niarchos would forgather with Dewi Soekarno, Günther Sachs, the Agnellis and Joan Collins. But it was on the banks of Lake Geneva, in a superbly magnificent setting, that their first child, Francesca, nicknamed 'Chessie', and her brother Lorne, were born, in 1958 and 1963 respectively. Fiona, who was listed as one of the Eight Most Elegant Women in Europe, was the subject of a major photo report only a few months before the birth of her son, where she was shown beside the other seven: Marella Agnelli, Patricia Lopez-Willshaw, Tina Onassis (Marchioness of Blandford), Princess Grace, Dolores Guinness, Countess Consuelo Crespi and Princess Lee Radziwill. Philippe Halsman photographed her wearing a maternity dress in the grounds of the villa and, in one of the splendid galleries, in a silk ensemble designed by Princess Irene Galitzine. Despite her outward serenity, she gave an impression of distance and melancholy.

It may be that the pictures offered a foretaste of what was to come; the Thyssens were divorced in 1964. Fiona obtained custody of her children and left Switzerland to live in London. Early in the seventies, she thought she could rebuild her life with Alexander Onassis, son of the famous shipowner. They grew so close that it appeared that nothing could separate them. But in January 1973, Alexander was killed in a flying accident.

Nothing has ever mattered more to Fiona than the happiness of her children. Today, Lorne lives in London where he is an actor. As for Francesca, after studying art history, she concentrated on organizing exhibitions at the Villa Favorita. She also set up ARCH (Art Restoration for Cultural Heritage), in order to safeguard the artistic wealth of East Europe. On Sunday January 31, 1993, at Mariazell, in Austria, she married Archduke Karl de Habsbourg-Lorraine. For several weeks, Fiona was exclusively preoccupied with preparations for the great ball which took place the day before the religious ceremony, in the Benedictine monastery of Gaming, attended by 600 people. It was an ideal occasion to reunite all the members of the family, together with prestigious guests, like the Princes of Savoie, Princess Gloria von Thurn und Taxis, Queen Anne of Romania and the Duke of Argyll. Assured of her children's well-being, Fiona has devoted herself for some years to animal welfare; she is said to be as effective in this field in Britain as Brigitte Bardot in France.

Barbara Goalen

In the late 1940s, Barbara Goalen was the first in Great Britain to raise modelling to the level of a respectable profession.

Early in her career, however, she had some problems in gaining the confidence of the fashion magazines. As Jean Dawnay recalls in her memoirs, *Model Girl*: 'The uncrowned queen of the models, and the centre of a whirl of publicity, was Barbara Goalen . . . It was by no means plain sailing for Barbara to arrive at her exalted position. There were difficultites to be overcome, like her aristocratic nose which cast bad shadows in photographs, and had to be made more photogenic by means of plastic surgery . . . It was a wonderful investment. Her incredibly slender bones, long graceful hands and superbly elegant way of posing made her a leading model. Since her retirement many models have tried to take her place but nobody has quite achieved it.' She was exceptionally photogenic, while at the same time possessing the ease and presence of a great lady, on whom a simple cotton blouse looked as though it had come direct from Dior. This combination of qualities was very rare. When you saw her in the pages of a magazine, she always seemed to have been photographed in her own clothes. Before her, no Englishwoman had been called on by France *Vogue* to cover the collections with photographers like Robert Randall, Arik Népo, Don Honeyman and Horst. One could hardly have a better recommendation than that. Thoughout her career she embodied a form of distant and inaccessible sophistication, which was the quintessence of elegance in the 1950s. Her contribution to the world of fashion was inestimable. While forming a legendary duo with John French, she successfully launched in Britain the wave of 'women of the world' models, which had a decisive influence on fashion photography.

The press christened her 'The Got-It Girl', or 'La Goalen' (as one might say 'La Callas'): Barbara had 'star quality'. In her view, it was not just a matter of posing in a dress but of giving it a life of its own; that is to say, understanding the context in which a particular outfit might be chosen so that one could wear it in a consistent and correct manner. Isn't elegance, more than anything else, the achievement of harmony between a given situation, a personality and a set of clothes? This innate sense of what a model should ideally represent scored heavily with the public. As a result, on a promotional journey abroad, when she had to take part in press conferences to explain her tastes in fashion, hordes of hysterical fans would be waiting for her wherever she went, making it difficult for her to move. The police even had to be called in to calm them down.

One had to admire Barbara's love of her work, which was, to say the least, disinterested. In the early 1950s, the salary of even the most famous models in Great Britain was in no way comparable to what one could earn at the same time in the United States. One would suppose that she was the best rewarded of her generation in Britain, yet she was only paid five guineas an hour for posing and two guineas for a day with *Vogue*. As a result, she had to work constantly and accepted this so that she could live entirely from it. Of course, it was not a bad life. Barbara only ever travelled in a chauffered Rolls Royce, and bunches of flowers, vintage champagne and fine chocolates greeted her at every stop. She was so appreciative of these kind attentions that she forgot the rest. In such a privileged environment, one can understand her dislike of the weekend, which was synonymous with idleness and a relapse into the everyday world. She always waited impatiently for Monday to come around, when she could set off for the studio.

It is impossible to speak of Barbara Goalen's career without mentioning that of John French, whom she inspired, becoming his most famous model. In April 1952, the *Daily Express* published an article on the ten greatest models of the year. John French naturally took the photographs of Barbara, along with Shelagh Wilson, Myrtle Crawford, Sylvia Shelley, Joan Burgess, Pat Squires, June Clarke, Pat Goddard, Susan Hook and June Duncan. Goalen and French started to work together in 1948. At that time, Barbara, now a widow who had to bring up her two children on her own, had joined a fashion house as a model. As soon as they met, he knew immediately that she would rise to become one of the very greatest. French, who had failed to make a living as an illustrator, had gone into fashion photography a little under ten years earlier: the *Daily Express* was the first to make use of his work in 1936. Since then, he had established himself as one of the most refined photographers of his time. Barbara and he had a perfect understanding, and there are numerous examples of the inspired chemistry between them in *Vogue, Vanity Fair, The Daily Express* and *The Tatler.* Both of them showed wit and subtelty in every situation: they might have stepped directly out of a play by Noel Coward. French, like Cecil Beaton and later Tony Armstrong-Jones, was a true gentleman whose quiet elegance Barbara much appreciated. He had a knack, more than anyone else, for immortalizing her slightly arrogant beauty which faintly recalled that of the unforgettable Kay Kendall. Barbara might have danced all night, as she liked to do, but nothing would make her miss one of their photo sessions. As soon as she entered his studio, she left weariness and worries behind her, as if by magic, and devoted herself exclusively to work. Her magnetic personality also inspired other photographers, including Cecil Beaton, Henry Clarke (who took some exceptionally lovely photographs of her in clothes by Balenciaga in 1949), Norman Parkinson and Richard Dormer, whom she helped to achieve an international reputation. We should also mention that Barbara was one of the favourite models of Clifford Coffin, who is now unjustly forgotten. A versatile and aggressive genius, he could light a face better than anyone; but, despite his highly original talent, his verbal and physical violence scared many people off. He would not hesitate to eject fashion editors from his studio and terrified young women. It was not unusual for him to try to transform them according to some fancy, forcing them to change their hairstyles or shave their eyebrows, to bring them closer to his latest vision of ideal femininity. Needless to say, they would emerge 'disfigured' and unable to find work again for weeks. He behaved very differently towards Barbara, whom he greatly admired. Appreciating her strong personality, he did not try to change her but photographed her as she was.

Despite her fame, Barbara Goalen retired at the height of her success, in 1956, to marry Nigel Campbell, an underwriter at Lloyds. Her admirers waited for hours outside Caxton Hall, where the wedding took place, to see her in her bridal dress. Five years later, these same admirers, inconsolable and nostalgic, saw her again in the tribute organized by the *Daily Express* to mark her 25 years of fruitful collaboration with John French. He posed for Terence Donovan beside the women who, throughout those years, had been his greatest models. Barbara Goalen was prominent among them, as well as Shelagh Wilson, Jean Dawnay, Jennifer Hockings, Shirley Worthington, Celia Hammond, Tania Mallet, Patti Boyd, Paulene Stone and others.

Dovima
© Henry Clarke, 1956, ADAGP, Paris and DACS, London 1995

Denise Sarrault, Monte-Carlo, 1960
© Jeanloup Sieff

Lisa Fonssagrives-Penn
© Paris Match Archives/Irving Penn

Mimi d'Arcangues
© Elle Archives/J.-F. Clair

Capucine
© X. (D.R.), with the kind permission
of the Givenchy Archives, Paris

Bettina
© X. (D.R.), with the kind permission
of the Givenchy Archives, Paris

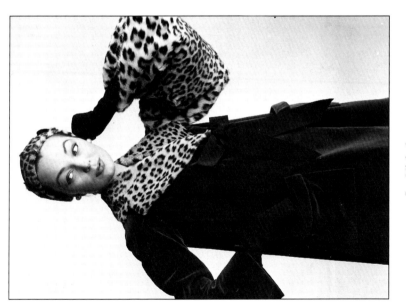

Ivy Nicholson
© Pierre Balmain, with the kind permission
of the Balmain Archives, Paris

Dorian Leigh with her sister, Susy Parker
© Paris Match Archives/Willy Rizzo

Susy Parker
© Paris Match Archives/Willy Rizzo

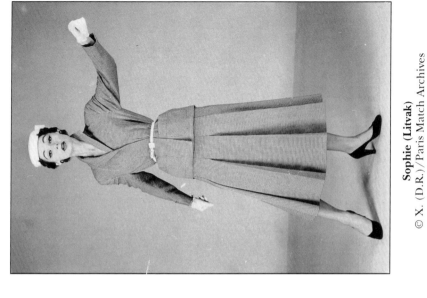

Sophie (Litvak)
© X. (D.R.)/Paris Match Archives

Simone d'Aillencourt
© Pierre Balmain, with the kind permission
of the Balmain Archives, Paris

Victoire, in a bridal gown, with Yves Saint Laurent
and, on the right, the model Christine
© Paris Match Archives/Willy Rizzo

Marie-Hélène Arnaud and Mademoiselle Chanel
© Paris Match Archives/Roger Picherie

Viviane Porte-Deblème
© X. (D.R.)

Hiroko Matsumoto
© Paris Match Archives/De Mervellec

Fiona Campbell-Walter
© X. (D.R.), Paris Match Archives

Jean Shrimpton
© Paris Match Archives/Patrice Habans

Anne Gunning
© Henry Clarke, 1952, ADAGP, Paris

Barbara Goalen
© Paris Match Archives/René Vital

Solange
© X. (D.R.), with the kind permission
of the Balenciaga Archives, Paris

Alla
© Paris Match Archives/J.-P. Pedrazzini

Liane
© Archives Marie-Claire/M. Jarnoux

Marie-Thérèse
© Pierre Balmain, with the kind permission
of the Balmain Archives, Paris

Praline
© Pierre Balmain, with the kind permission
of the Balmain Archives, Paris

Bronwen Pugh
© Pierre Balmain, with the kind permission
of the Balmain Archives, Paris

Anne Saint-Marie
© Henry Clarke, 1955, ADAGP, Paris

Anne Gunning

Anne Gunning occupies a quite exceptional place in the fashion photography of the 1950s. Pre-Raphaelite madonna, mournful pierrot, her diaphanous charm was combined with a very 'Black Irish' touch which she owed to her mother. She had a powerful appeal for many in the world of fashion: Henry Clarke, who discovered her; Richard Dormer, who consistently worked with her; and the dressmaker Sybil Connolly, for whom she became a favourite client and a close friend. To all those who at some time or other had the privilege of working with her, Anne Gunning undoubtedly remains one of the most enchanting beauties of her generation.

Her childhood was spent on the huge African estate of her father, a Scottish expatriate. Like dozens of teenagers in the postwar period, she wanted to become an actress. She came to

London and was hired by the Rank Organization, which since 1946 had taken over the main film companies in the country, as well as the studios at Pinewood and Denham, and she was soon to join the large number of young women whom the group kept in reserve, idly waiting for parts. 'She has a withdrawn, Garbo-like quality', Jean Dawnay observed, 'and I am sure that if she had continued in the film career that she started with the Rank Organization, today she would be one of the loveliest actresses on the screen. A director has only to look at the way she poses and her expression in a photograph to see how responsive she is to the camera.' One day, when she was having dinner in a smart restaurant in the King's Road, the photographer Henry Clarke came up and asked her if she would pose for him. Reassured by his manner, Anne, who was just 18 and had never thought of becoming a model, accepted his proposal without hesitation. They took their first photos together for *Harper's Bazaar*, and the young woman was launched.

In a matter of a few weeks, the leading fashion photographers wanted her to pose for them. After Clarke, with whom she would continue to work throughout her career, it was the turn of John French, whose collaboration with the famous model Barbara Goalen was universally admired. In Britain, posing for him would make a model's name. He fully appreciated the different facets of Anne's personality and knew how to bring them out. In the course of time, he would transform her into a mysterious and vulnerable stranger, her face hidden behind a veil for the British edition of *Harper's Bazaar* in October 1950; into a dramatic beauty (for an advertising campaign commissioned by Harvey Nichols), dressed in a magnificent evening coat in British *Vogue* in December 1952; or an ingénue, fresh faced and laughing, to show off Dior's new 'A-line' for *Vanity Fair* in May 1955. French's wife, impressed by such professionalism, had the idea of recommending Anne to Richard Dormer, a young photographer who had been noticed by Ernestine Carter, who was at that time an editor of the English edition of *Harper's*. She guessed that their talents would complement each other perfectly. Never has anyone been proved more correct.

Anne Gunning and Richard Dormer made a particularly inspired pair as model and photographer. For Dormer, Anne was the ideal woman: splendidly photogenic, yet with an unusual type of beauty, fitting no stereotype. Cultivated, full of humour and reserve, she always understood precisely what was required of her, notably in moments of crisis — a fact well illustrated in an anecdote told by Charles Castle. In the course of one of their many journeys around the world for *Harper's Bazaar*, a television crew was accompanying them to Bangkok to make a documentary on their methods of work. The episode was not entirely problem-free. Dormer wanted very soft lighting, to evoke the softly padded and peaceable side of his aesthetic world, while the TV technicians were asking for a much cruder form of lighting in order to obtain pictures of the best possible quality. This difference in approach made things considerably more complicated, and it was agreed that there should be two photo sessions every time, one for Dormer, the other for the television crew. This doubling of the work very quickly put them a long way behind their original schedule, and this began to get on the photographer's nerves. The situation was made worse by the personality of the fashion editor in charge of the report, who was constantly unable to make up her mind about which dress and accessories should be worn. Inevitably, Dormer took out his frustrations on Anne and the quarrel that ensued was exceptionally violent: they worked together for a whole week without speaking a word to one another. The atmosphere was electric, the tension palpable. Yet the results were astonishing, because the pair could understand one another without the need for words. Yet, this kind of dispute, which was inevitable between two such strong personalities, did not at all alter their unshakeable friendship.

While Anne had a particularly close relationship with Richard Dormer, she did also work with many other photographers, including Skilford, Beaton, Randall, Prigent, Rawlings, Pottier and William Klein — and the extravagant Norman Parkinson. Though each of them, in his own way, was able to appreciate her qualities, it was undoubtedly Parkinson who was among those who most fully sensed the intensity of her presence. For the record, one may recall the journey they made to India in the Autumn of 1956 for *Vogue*. He photographed her in the Palace of Jaipur, in a setting drenched in different tones of pink, each one more expressive than the next: a perfect foil to her elegant pallor. It was a complete success. When Diana Vreeland saw these photos, she wittily remarked: 'How clever of you, Mr Parkinson, to have realized that in India, pink is the local navy blue!'

Of course, Anne appeared more than once on the cover of the bible of haute couture. It is hardly surprising that all the most famous brands of cosmetics, from Helena Rubenstein to Revlon, called on her services convinced that her radiant presence would bring more to their advertising than that of any other famous cover girl.

Unlike some great models, who find it amusing to take part in the presentation of a collection, Anne Gunning always turned down offers of that kind — with one exception. Just once, she did agree to appear on the catwalk for her friend Sybil Connolly, the greatest Irish designer of the day. Connolly, who had started at the age of seventeen to train in the subtleties of the dressmaker's art with Bradley's (one of the most famous fashion houses of the 1930s), showed her first personal collection in the United States in 1952. It resulted in a lyrical article in *Time* magazine and six pages in *Life*, including the cover. Later, in 1957, Sybil established her own fashion house in Dublin where she made a name for imaginative and refined creations. Anne Gunning, who always greatly admired her, set aside her misgivings and modelled one of her collections. And yet, at the same time, all the most famous couturiers had been pestering her to appear as the star of one of their press shows. Even Mademoiselle Chanel got in touch with her personally, after sending her a photograph of herself which had been taken many years before by Horst, saying that she found a striking resemblance between the two of them. Chanel liked to choose her models in such a way as to evoke an echo of her own former beauty: this was especially true of the Brazilian Vera Valdez, her 'double', whom she brought to Paris at great expense for a single collection. However, she never managed to persuade Anne. It was 'Mademoiselle's' only failure.

At the start of the 1960s, Anne Gunning brought her outstanding career to an end in order to marry Anthony Nutting. Having served under one of Britain's most exceptional Prime

Ministers, as a prominent member of Sir Anthony Eden's cabinet, Nutting was a specialist in Middle Eastern affairs, while at the same time a skilled diplomat and an established man of letters. His essay on the political role played by T. E. Lawrence is a definitive work. However, his wife did not entirely give up the world of fashion. From time to time she agreed to pose in a creation by her friend Sybil Connolly, as she did, for example, in March 1962, for French *Vogue*, photographed by Henry Clarke. One can hardly imagine a more brilliant ambassador's wife. Lady Nutting died in January, 1990.

Jean Shrimpton

The most talented fashion photographers will tell you that it was impossible ever to take a bad photo of her; legend has it that even her passport photo could have featured on the cover of *Vogue*! Jean Shrimpton, however, was much more than just an outstanding cover girl. She summed up the aesthetic aspirations of a whole decade, the 1960s, and became the symbol of the ideal woman for an entire generation. Her age fell in love with her face, finding in it the image that would satisfy all its fantasies. She was so famous, and so adored, from 1961 onwards, that at the age of 23 she had already published a book of memoirs, *My Own Story: the Truth About Modelling* in 1965, which was a bestseller, and a film, *The Face on the Cover*, had just been made about her work. Meanwhile, American clothing companies were, for the first time, launching a tailor's dummy with the features and measurements of the great model. The facts speak for themselves: Jean was five feet, eight-and-a-half inches tall, and weighed one hundred and eighteen pounds. Her vital stastistics were thirty-four, twenty-four, thirty-five. Everything has been said and written about her: her make-up, her tastes, her private life and her influence on fashion photography. But Cecil Beaton best defined the magic of Jean Shrimpton, which has still not been equalled: 'She is the unicorn, the rare creature, almost mythical'.

Jean Shrimpton was born on November 6, 1942, in the heart of the English countryside. Her father was in business, her mother was a housewife; she had one sister, Chrissie, a brother, Danny, and lived on a farm with horses. Her schooling was conventional, almost dull. Obviously, if you like to believe in destiny, there were already signs which might suggest that as a baby she would one day be exceptionally beautiful. Throughout her childhood, local photographers and painters vied for the honour of immortalizing the little girl, whose large clear eyes already fascinated all those who met her and were soon to make her famous. At sixteen, not wanting to stay at school for ever, this very conventional young Englishwoman took time out to laze for a while, spending her time either riding or at social events (where her arrival would invariably attract the cameras), then decided to take a secretarial course. It was not an especially original move, but a sensible one for a young woman who wanted to achieve financial independence quickly. In the midst of this dull period, while attending a polo match at Windsor Castle in 1958, Jean was presented to the dressmaker Norman Hartnell, who was a guest in the royal box. His fashion house, at 26 Burton Street, was famous for belonging to the official dressmaker to the royal family. A theatre lover, Hartnell had studied at Cambridge and created the ceremonial robes for Queen Elizabeth II's coronation in 1953 and her wedding dress in 1947. Jean posed for a photographer that same day and, a short while later, saw her picture in the popular magazine *Woman's Own*. Fate, as we know, never leaves anything to chance, and it had shown its hand. Next, it was the turn of the film-maker Cyril Enfield, who came up to her outside her secretarial school and offered her a part in his next film, *Mysterious Island.* She knew nothing about acting, but her presence was miraculous, and Enfield firmly believed that the movie camera would succumb to her magnetism. But it would have been much too simple for the young country girl to become a star after just one film! Fate (again) abhors a cliché: Jean was being saved for quite a different future. As it turned out, the film's producer refused to hire her and Enfield, in consternation, advised her to go along to Lucie Clayton, the top London model agency. This move was to change her life.

After taking the course which the agency gave to every new recruit, Jean was soon free to pose. Her range was extremely varied, allowing her to work for employers as different as British *Vogue* and mail order catalogues: the latter first gave her the opportunity to travel. From the artistic point of view, the crucial step in her career was her meeting with John French, which was both a turning-point in her professional life (since he was able to get Jean's pictures into the leading magazines), and in her personal life. At that time his young assistant was David Bailey. It was thanks to John French, who was very elegant and well bred, that all the young lions of fashion photography in the 1960s, such as Bailey, Terence Donovan and Brian Duffy, who had almost all come from the poor districts of the East End of London, managed to get their first big break. French was able to perceive the real potential behind their apparent uncouthness.

The legendary association between Jean Shrimpton and David Bailey began while the latter was still working with French. The English edition of *Vogue* commissioned his first fashion assignment and he naturally chose Jean as his model. It was love at first sight. In a hard-working and, at the same time, intensely erotic atmosphere, the two really got to know one another. Jean soon capitulated to his energy and tenacity, which swept everything before them. Since he had very little in the way of culture or education, he could sometimes appear boorish, but she loved him because he was himself whatever the circumstances, with his cockney humour, his strong sense of self-mockery and his arrogant manner. At the photographer's request, she always called him simply: 'Bailey'. As for Bailey himself, he found in her his alter ego, his muse and a great gentleness which helped to calm his own excessive aggression. In 1961, Jean Shrimpton really became an international star when Bailey photographed her for a story in the series 'The Young Idea'. This new column in British *Vogue* was concerned with more unaffected and easily available clothes, shown by younger and less sophisticated models posing in more natural settings; a foretaste of the rising tide of ready-to-wear clothes which nothing could now stem. It was Bailey's idea to immortalize her beside people, like Vidal Sassoon and Dudley Moore, whose creative efforts were to establish the enduring image of 'Swinging London'. This first assignment was such a success that they were asked to go to New York for the same series. Between a recital by Ella Fitzgerald and a meeting with Dali, he photographed her, without misgivings, in the heart of Harlem! Until then this harsh and persecuted world had always been kept strictly under wraps. Now it appeared in all its raw reality on the pages of the most élitist of fashion magazines. The visual shock was to steer an entire generation of photographers in an entirely new direction, and the repercussions would last throughout the decade.

Jean Shrimpton's great strength lay in the fact that her beauty was simultaneously chameleon-like and immediately identifiable. A strong personality, imitated and envied throughout the world, lending itself to any situation, was a dream for fashion photographers and editors. She could as easily represent the ideal of young people in the first half of the '60s when she posed for 'The Young Idea' or in *Elle**, as show off the collections of the great Parisian couturiers in her own inimitable style. Very soon, barely a year after the start of her career as a model, Jean was already being recognized in the street and besieged with requests for interviews from the press. With David Bailey, she was constantly in demand both professionally and privately. There were trips to New York to work with Diana Vreeland,

---

* Jean worked a lot for the French weekly, often appearing on the cover: her fans could admire her playing tennis (10 June 1965), in haute couture twinset (12 June 1964), in a spring evening gown with the caption 'Most Beautiful Woman in the World' (27 May 1965), as an Amazon in Havana suede (22 November 1963) or swamped in waves of red fox (13 September 1963) — to mention only a few of her covers for *Elle*.

ducking and bobbing to dodge the paparazzi on both sides of the Atlantic, invitations to talk shows and parties of every sort.

From an artistic point of view, London had become the centre of the world and seemed on the brink of some great upheaval. Bailey was tireless and determined to enjoy every last drop of his sudden success, so he was constantly taking her to fashionable nightspots like the Saddle Room or the Ad Lib. Jean hated these crowded, noisy places. As soon as they arrived, she would find a quiet corner and take out her knitting! The almost surreal image of the famous *Vogue* model with two needles and a ball of wool on her lap, pressed between one of the Beatles and Julie Christie, drove Bailey mad. Jean much preferred the picturesque life, full of homely fun, that they spent with their two dogs and 24 birds, far from the madding crowd. In fact, through all these years, she only ever owned one evening dress, a black jersey sheath by the American couturier, Rudy Gernreich.

After working exclusively together for some time, Jean and Bailey decided to branch out a bit, to avoid getting into a rut. Jean was now free to pose for Henry Clarke. She did her first cover for French *Vogue* with him in April 1963, in a Dior dress. That same year, she made the cover of French *Vogue* twice more in succession, but this time with Bailey: first in October, in a tweed coat lined with beaver by Chanel; and then in November in an outfit by Yves Saint Laurent. Cecil Beaton took a photograph of her in 1964 which has become legendary, in the style of an eighteenth-century marquise with powdered wig and beauty spot, her perfect profile silhouetted against an abstract background. She was asked to model for Irving Penn, Jeanloup Sieff, Guy Bourdin, Fouli Elia, William Klein — and Richard Avedon, who she thought had a special knack (like John French) of making women look incredibly beautiful. In her second volume of memoirs, *An Autobiography*, published in 1990, she describes with a great deal of humour how Avedon had the odd habit of making a collage if he wasn't pleased with every part of a model's body; so Jean found photographs of herself where only the face was hers, the hands and, in some cases, the whole body, having been replaced!

After her break with Bailey, Jean had a brief and bizarre affair with the disconcerting actor Terence Stamp, which was founded on a clash of temperaments as the result of insurmountable communication problems and a hectic social life. 'The two most beautiful human beings in London,' their friend Cyril Enfield would say of them. It was a strange period. Jean, the cover girl most in demand in the whole world, was even offered diamonds in a bowl of rice by one of her most ardent admirers in one of the most fashionable Chinese restaurants in London.

Quite involuntarily, she caused a scandal during a trip to Australia. She was invited to award the 1965 Melbourne Gold Cup, which she did, in a white mini-skirt, suntanned, with bare legs and no hat or gloves, at what was the most formal occasion in the Australian social calendar. There was a general outcry, but she helped to popularize the mini-skirt, which up to than had been slow to catch on.

So famous was she that by 1966, she was being offered film parts. That year she played a painter in *Privilege*, a film by Peter Watkins, where she co-starred with the singer Paul Jones, who was playing a pop star, manipulated by both the Church and the Government. But Jean was always aware of her potential, and also of her limitations; she never felt she had it in her to be an actress. She did however, at this time, almost make a film with Michael Cacoyannis and did a screen test for him in Greece. Could the director of *Zorba the Greek* have revealed a new star with a real screen presence to the world? No one will ever know, because Candice Bergen got the part. Meanwhile, her life as a model was still as busy. Hardly pausing to draw breath, she hurried from a cruise on Stavros Niarchos' boat 'The Creole', where for ten days she made a highly seductive couple with Jeanloup Sieff — purely for the sake of a photo assignment which appeared in the January 1967 American *Vogue* — to an exclusive three-year contract with Yardley. This contract, which only applied to the advertising of hair products in the United States, was exceptional in more ways than one. At £70,000, a fortune for the sixties, it involved advertising shots and promotional campaigns for magazines, under the aegis of the great photographer Melvin Sokolsky, as well as press conferences, twice a year for a fortnight, throughout the country. Jean had undoubtedly arrived.

In 1969, Jean Shrimpton, the most famous model in the world, decided to retire. She was 26, had travelled all around the world, met fascinating people, worn superb clothes and posed for an untold number of magazine covers, while being handsomely rewarded for her time! There was no way that she would agree to be anything less than the best, so even though she was more than ever in demand, Jean decided to anticipate the inevitable. She left London and bought a delapidated hotel in Wales where she could take up photography, this time working behind the lens. From time to time, whenever she was offered some really exceptional job, she would agree to come back: an American TV commercial for Avedon, a trip to Egypt with Bailey for *Vogue*, and a fashion show — the only one she ever did — in Turkey, where she was the star. Nothing less. At the end of the 1970s, she moved to Cornwall where she opened an antique shop. A keen lover of art — at the time when *Privilege* was released, she started an art collection by buying two Egon Schieles — and of decoration. Thanks to her friend Geoffrey Bennison, Jean had trained her eye, while not denigrating her own very sure individual taste. It was in her shop that she met Michael, her future husband, who had come as a customer — a calm, quiet man, who could at last offer her all the inner strength that she had so long sought. On January 12, 1979, Jean Shrimpton, 35, one of the loveliest faces of the century, became Mrs Michael Cox. Since that time they have lived in a hotel in Penzance, bringing up their son Thaddeus. Jean later agreed to do one more advertising campaign, solely to restore the roof of the Abbey Hotel; something which was to bring comfort to the minds of many older women suffering the agony of their first grey hairs.

An interview with Jeanloup Sieff

Jeanloup Sieff rarely uses the word '*photo*'; he prefers the more evocative term '*image*'. His work, which mixes poetry with a hint of nostalgia and a great deal of humour, has borne witness to the events of more than four decades with an insight that remains true, whatever the subject of his photographs. A famous model, a writer, a dancer, a miners' strike, the Scottish highlands or the funeral of Pope Pius XII: Jeanloup Sieff's talent was not devoted solely to the service of fashion. Even when he was doing a daily photo session for the American edition of *Vogue* or for *Elle*, he never minded dropping it for a month to compile a dossier on Auschwitz or a report on the Polish elections. As well as the most prestigious women's magazines, he also regularly contributed to *Life* and *Réalités*. In 1958, he even joined the Magnum agency for a year.

In the 1950s, he brought his experience as a great reporter to the world of fashion photography, preferring to get away from the confined space of the studio to bring his models into the outside world. The women whom he immortalized were more restrained in their gestures and more subtle in their make-up; and, for that very reason, exhaled a quiet sense of class and a timeless beauty, shunning clichés and excess.

It is hardly surprising that the most demanding of art directors put all their trust in him. His record speaks for itself: *Vogue, Harper's Bazaar, Glamour, Queen, Femme, Nova, Elle* and *Jardin des Modes*: all of them called on his services.

For him, Denise Sarrault, Enid Boulting and Jean Shrimpton —the most famous models — were transformed into heroines: either fragile, melancholy or sensual, but always sensitive and vital. A beautiful '*image*' is, above all, a story and a feeling.

When did you take your first fashion photograph?

S: In 1952, when I was in my last year at school. I went up to a young woman in the street: she was called Rose-Marie Le Quellec and was a star model at Fath's. It all happened very naturally.

Some photographers prefer to work with their favourite models. This was true of John French and Barbara Goalen, Richard Dormer and Anne Gunning, or David Bailey and Jean Shrimpton, to mention only the best known. In the 1950s and 1960s, did you have a favourite?

S: When I think about it, I photographed very different models, but as far as possible always tried to choose women who appealed to me personally — not just in their looks, but more because I needed to get on with them. But I never had an exclusive model, like Penn and his wife, Lisa Fonssagrives. There was one girl with whom I worked a lot, especially for *Harper's*: she was a German called Ina. We made some fine pictures together.

In her Autobiography, *Jean Shrimpton says that she was very disturbed and attracted by you in your first photo session. Were you helped*

or motivated by this relationship between the artist and the model, that
ambiguous and sensual chemistry?

S: You might say that the choice of subject and the rapport that
I established with her were really the only things that made me
want to work with one model rather than another, regardless of
whether the attraction was physical or intellectual. It's like
making a portrait: it will only be a success if one has an affinity
with the person who is posing for you. I have made many
portraits of writers, and the best images were the ones that I
made of those whom I admire. The relationship with a model is
very similar. This is why one often comes across pairings of
models and photographers.

What do you understand by the term 'photogenic'?

S: I once had a long discussion with Maurice Béjart [the French
dancer and choreographer] about this.We came to the conclu-
sion that someone photogenic doesn't necessarily fit the canons
of so-called classical beauty. Physical appearance is not everything, even though it is clear that some faces catch the light
better than others. It's chiefly the projection of an inner life.
    I have met with many disappointments. I've seen magnificent
girls with whom I really wanted to work, then after the trial
shots, I realized that their look was quite empty, like a very
beautiful, but uninhabited apartment. On the other hand,
there are women who were outstanding models and who showed
themselves to be utterly insignificant in life. I'm thinking, for
example, of Nicole de La Margé. She had such a sense of light
and what was right for her that she actually became photogenic.
The opposite can happen. Some women appear both splendid
to look at and intelligent in daily life, but have no photogenic
qualities in front of the lens. They will never be great models.
It's a complete mystery.

So what are, in your view, the qualities of a great model, of a woman who
has stood out and made an impression on her time?

S: With some, it's the encounter between some physical trait, some inner life that she projects, and an age which is looking for itself and needs someone to crystallize it and reflect it. Thanks to this miraculous alchemy, the model is elevated to a symbol of womanhood for an entire generation. In the case of Shrimpton, it was obviously the Swinging Sixties. I think she is the most perfect example of that symbiosis of a personality and a period — just like Simone d'Aillencourt, whom I often enjoyed photographing, Bettina or Susy Parker: each of them, in her own way, illustrates the woman of the Fifties.

Who are the models with whom you most liked to work?

S: Ina, of course, but also Jill Kennington, a great English girl with whom I often worked for *Queen*; then Shrimpton, Denise Sarrault, Astrid, a German whom I photographed a lot in New York for *Harper's*, and Maria Solar, who was so beautiful.

Do you have any particular memories of working with Denise Sarrault, one of the unforgettable models of that time?

S: Denise, for me, recalls that trip we made in 1960 to Monte Carlo for *Jardin des Modes*. It was a sort of parody and tribute to Greta Garbo. The situation was quite unusual: we set off together without an editor or anyone else. Denise did her own hair and make-up and we chose the clothes together. There were fourteen suitcases! We set the whole thing up between us. I even borrowed a Rolls which I found standing in front of the casino. It was incredibly good fun! Afterwards, we worked together a lot. We covered the collections in Italy and New York for *Harper's*. She was really a fantastic model.

And Ivy Nicholson?

S: Quite incredible. One day, for *Elle*, Hélène Lazareff asked me to do an assignment on 'a completely mad American girl who is doing painting in Rome': those were her very words. It was Ivy Nicholson. So I set off to Rome to photograph her. It was a very picturesque session. She had set up her easel in the Piazza di Spagna and was painting the Spanish Steps, surrounded by a crowd of very over-excited Italian men. She was splendid.

Can you tell me about Hiroko Matsumoto, who also posed for you?

S: Yes, we worked very successfully together. I remember her fragility, her grace. She was very interesting to photograph. She was a mysterious, enigmatic person.

Wasn't Marie-Hélène Arnaud also one of your models?

S: Yes, several times, especially when I was first working for *Elle*. At that time, I worked a lot with very sophisticated girls like Marie-Hélène or Dorian Leigh, who was coming to the end of her career. Marie-Hélène was both a house model and a photo model, just like Denise Sarrault or Hiroko Matsumoto. I have a very clear memory of one three-week trip with her to Spain. Claude Brouet was the fashion editor who came with us. I photographed her in the arena during the bullfights. I have to acknowledge that she was an exceptionally talented live model, but in my view she was not very interesting as a photographic model. On the other hand, Arsac did make some very fine pictures of her.

You were one of the first to photograph Nico, long before she became a well-known model, then a star of the Underground. Did you often work with utterly unknown girls who afterwards became famous?

S: Oh, yes, certainly. Once at the time of the collections, I wanted to do a parody for *Harper's*, based on the relationship of the Beatles to their fans. I have an English friend who was the double of Paul McCartney. Opposite him, I wanted a typically English girl from Swinging London, to play the part of a groupie. Throughout the story, she had to run after the pseudo McCartney to ask for his autograph, showing off different clothes in each picture. So I held an audition in London to find the ideal model. It was Jane Birkin. She was only 19 and already very different from the rest.

In your view, what are the ideal conditions for creating a beautiful image?

S: I like to work alone, and in silence, indoors or out. As it happens, this has caused me a lot of problems, because I've always been in the habit of putting everyone out at the studio door. After agreeing with the fashion editor what we're going to do, I stay alone with the model. A photograph is an exchange between two people.

And what, in your opinion, is the quality of a great model?

S: Being able to say no. I remember one Swedish girl whom I photographed a lot in 1958-59. She was at the start of a tremendous career: she was really magnificent and appeared on all the covers. Once, when we were taking some photos in Morocco, she told me that she would go on posing until she had enough money to buy a house for her parents and then, after that, she would study to be a nurse. She was a model for two years and stopped at a time when she could have earned millions. She gave everything up from one day to the next and, when she had collected the money she needed, she vanished. I suppose she is probably working now in a hospital in Sweden. It's marvellous to have the strength to say no, just when you are so much in demand. 'The Shrimp' also had the courage to call a halt to everything, just as the Japanese were offering her huge contracts to advertise cosmetics. I have a lot of admiration for that.

PART TWO

SUPERMODELS

Introduction

Parisian haute couture in the postwar years was a constantly changing world. While some houses, such as Balmain in 1945, Dior in 1947, Cardin in 1951 and Givenchy in 1952, were started up successfully, it became obvious that most of the many great couturiers were unable to adapt to the economic climate of the new decade and had to close down. Lucien Lelong was the first, in 1948, followed by Molyneux in 1950, Piguet in 1951, Chaumont in 1952, Lafaurie, Callot Soeurs, Drecoll and Rochas in 1953, and Schiaparelli in 1954, to mention only a few. At the same time, however, there were others, in the wake of these successive closures, who managed to establish veritable empires, giving the world of high fashion an impetus that it had never known before. The case of Christian Dior speaks for itself: twenty-eight workshops, five buildings, 1,400 employees producing 12,000 items a year — and all this in barely ten years! A fashion house at that time was like a city within the city: couturier, assistant dressmakers, *chef de cabine*, dressers, administrative staff, first and second salesgirls, first and second workshop assistants, tailors, seamstresses and embroiderers — not forgetting the models, who were the uncontested sovereigns of these kingdoms of style.

Throughout the 1950s, the 'house' models of a few foreign fashion houses were true stars: this was the case with Dolores and Cynthia, associated with Norman Hartnell in London. They were, however, very much the exception compared with their Parisian counterparts. Each great couturier had one, if not several, favourite models, and the press as a whole closely followed their professional and private lives, reporting a change of hair style, attendance at a ball, and the arrival of a new admirer, who would be prudishly described as a 'fiancé'. But, in reality, all this show hid work that was intense, exhausting and often thankless.

How did they spend their time? In general, the month preceding each of the two annual collections was entirely devoted to 'modelling' sessions with the couturier, from around 10am to 8pm, and sometimes late into the night in the event of a last-minute rush. From one stage to the next, the model lived through the development of every collection, and all the successive versions of the clothes that she would have to show were tailored to fit her and had her first name written on a *bolduc* (a ribbon or tape) sewn into the dress. The more the model inspired her dressmaker, the larger the number of creations that she would have to present on the catwalk. As a result, the hours of modelling would sometimes stretch interminably, because the clothes would be revised, undone and remade until the dressmaker was entirely satisfied with them. These sessions became all the more demanding since the world of haute couture is always one season ahead: at the height of summer, the models spend their whole day dressed in woollens and furs! Finally, on the eve of D-Day, there was a dress rehearsal in the most feverish atmosphere imaginable: last-minute repairs, instructions to the person in charge of accessories, to the milliner, to the hairdresser, to the furrier and, above all, the final orders to the models themselves. After the show (the prestigious press shows attended by journalists, clients and sponsors from all around the world), the 'girls' still had two weeks of unremitting work ahead of them. In the morning, they posed for photographers and illustrators and, in the afternoon, they were back on the catwalks, sometimes twice in a day, for the benefit of the many buyers. After this fortnight, they only came in at 3pm for the daily shows intended for customers. However, this schedule was even heavier during the years of mid-season models: at the end of the 1940s and the beginning of the 1950s, the great couturiers would also prepare two mid-term collections, shown at the end of the Autumn and the beginning of the Summer. These consisted of revised and summary versions of the two main collections, at once synthesizing and toning down the tendencies introduced a few months earlier (not forgetting that some outfits would try to inaugurate the incoming fashion). However, bit by bit these shows disappeared: 'An extension of the time occupied by the seasons,' Christian Dior recalled in his memoirs, *Dior by Dior*, 'a shortage of specialized labour and amortization difficulties led to them being completely abandoned.'

In the literal sense the *cabine* (studio) was a room, usually narrow, shaped like a corridor, in which each model had her own appointed place, in front of a table with a mirror above it. In the figurative sense, the term *cabine* referred to all the models who worked for a particular couturier: between seven and twelve girls, as well as some 'free-lancers' in the event of a major show, a gala or a trip abroad. Each house had its own style of model, corresponding to the aesthetic of the designer in charge. At the same time, while responding to the creator's ideals, the *cabine* had also to be made up of different types of women in order to recreate an ideal image of each customer. Each *cabine* had its own codes — of humour, language and tradition. So it was that the very latest recruits would be put at the far end of the room and the veterans near the exit. As girls left, those remaining behind would move up a notch, vacating her chair for the next in line. But, of all the rituals, it was the baptism of the model that was most popular, becoming a veritable institution: Capucine, Praline, Lucky, Tulipe, Bijou — each was a heroine whose first name alone would inspire the dreams of their audience.

Finally, we must say something about the shows themselves. They took place in the salons of the fashion houses but there are unfortunately very few pictures of them. The order of presentation was very strictly laid down: suits, day wear, more formal afternoon dresses, cocktail dresses, short evening dresses, long evening dresses, gala dresses and, last of all, the inevitable wedding dress. Contrary to the custom nowadays, press shows took place without musical accompaniment. An announcer would state the model in French, then repeat the number in English. The order, the accompanying effects, the presentation and the accessories differed for each outfit. The models did not swing their hips or leap in the air, and they never burst out laughing. They glided along very slowly, turned round delicately, held the pose to allow the spectators time to admire the dress and then left at a slow and majestic pace, leaning slightly backwards in order to accentuate the curve of the hips and the bust.

THE GREAT COUTURE HOUSES AND
THEIR SUPERMODELS

Cristobal Balenciaga

In her 1984 volume of memoirs *DV*, Diana Vreeland tells how one day, when she was at Mona Bismarck's on Capri, Consuelo Crespi called from Rome to announce the 'dreadful' news: Balenciaga had just closed his fashion house for good without warning anyone, even his most illustrious client and ambassador, the very elegant Bunny Mellon. Mona Bismarck, another great fan of the divine Cristobal, was so devastated that she refused to leave her room for three days.

Cristobal Balenciaga was much more than simply a talented creator. For many, he remains the greatest couturier of the century. Spanish by origin, he set up his first fashion business in 1914 in San Sebastian, then went successively to Madrid and Barcelona before leaving his native country at the time of the Civil War in 1936. But Balenciaga is chiefly celebrated for the clothes that he created between 1937 and 1968 in his workshops in the Avenue George-V. A mysterious figure, he always refused to be interviewed. It appeared that all that mattered to him was a continuing search for perfection. One has only to think of his scarf jacket, his kimono coats, his evening dresses with a 'poof' effect achieved by resting the material on the hips, his 'sack' dresses, his lace 'baby-dolls' and his ceaseless efforts to create the ideal sleeve — the fruit of a painstaking geometrical study. All of these unforgettable creations were worn with exceptional style by the Duchess of Montesquiou-Fezensac, Gloria Guinness or Marlene Dietrich and, years later, by Tina Chow.

People often speak of austere elegance, even of severity, when they mention his dresses, because Balenciaga avoided any gratuitous ornamentation and anything that might disturb the purity of the line. This same element of sobriety was also often to be found in his favourite colours — black, a tribute to his Spanish origins, and all the darker tones in general; and yet he was capable of transforming his collections into fantastic firework displays. Everyone still remembers his magnificent violets: pink and blue-tinged. His only detectable concessions to luxury were sumptuously embroidered boleros for evening wear and wispy lace dresses. Finally, like most couturiers, Balenciaga launched his own scents: *Le Dix* (1947), *La Fuite des Heures* (1948), *Quadrille* (1955) and *Ho Hang* (1971).

His integrity and his fidelity to beauty and refinement were what led him in 1968 to close the doors of his Parisian dressmaking business for the last time in order to avoid having to make concessions to the demands of an age which he considered second-rate. A year later (three years before his death), he did the same with his Madrid salons. In 1992, a thirty-year old Dutchman, Josephus Melchior Thimister, took on the demanding task of reviving the brilliance and lustre of the house of Balenciaga.

Solange

What woman has never dreamed of being the leading model and inspiration of the great Cristobal Balenciaga? To see him create, day by day for eighteen years, those extraordinary dresses, which are today eagerly displayed in museums, while embodying his definition of elegance, season after season, in the eyes of the world? It would be an unforgettable lesson in discipline and perfection. This was the role that Solange played for the designer with immense joy and, she would gladly say, with immense pride too.

It all began in 1939, when a friend who was a model at Patou's advised her to try her luck with a fashion house herself. Amused by the idea, Christiane (she was only to abandon her true name when she arrived at Balenciaga's, because another model already had it), went first to Molyneux and then to Maggy Rouff.

She was immediately attracted to the quietly luxurious atmosphere in which she now found herself, but after only a few months the war put an abrupt end to this promising career. After the Liberation, wanting to drive away her memory of the years of sadness and austerity, she decided to return to the ideal world of Parisian haute couture and knocked at the door of Balenciaga, at No 10, Avenue George-V. The designer hired her on the spot, and an hour later she had started to work for him.

The Balenciaga *cabine* was very different from all the rest. The Master did not like the 'star' side of models who appeared on the front pages of magazines either in a professional or a private capacity. He found that sort of thing a bit flashy for his taste. His hallmarks were always discretion and reserve. In Balenciaga's view, a model should inspire the couturier and exhibit his work to its best advantage, with grace and balance. The last thing he wanted was for anyone to overlook the clothes and concentrate on the person wearing them. Solange stresses that the *cabine* reflected the image of the artist. There was no social life and a lot of endless hard work. The few occasional moments of intimacy were enjoyed as a family matter. Balenciaga, who put fidelity above everything, always worked with the same six or seven 'girls' whom he knew well and in whom he had absolute confidence. Unlike so many other couturiers, he did not encourage the vogue for temporary or freelance models which was to come in during the late 1950s.

Solange perfectly embodied the Balenciaga woman: reassuringly human. The clients could easily see themselves in her and, consequently, in the clothes she was showing. This was not always the case with other women — such as Praline at Balmain's, or Alla and Lucky at Dior's — whose theatrical beauty always inspired admiration but often prevented any form of identification. The same concern for purity and sobriety was to be found in the hair and make-up. Solange remembers that Balenciaga detested any kind of excess in either of these. She would arrive at the studio in the morning, hardly made up at all, and with her hair neatly drawn back into an irreproachable chignon; she admits that she never even wore the false eyelashes that were so much in fashion. However, while the Master always demanded reserve, patience and punctuality from his models, the rewards were equal to the effort. Solange wore his most famous creations, from his tunic dresses to his kimono coats. For the Coronation of Queen Elizabeth II, he even invented a court dress for her with train and diadem. This was one of Solange's favourite ensembles. At the time of the collections, Balenciaga was always absorbed in thought and invariably absent-minded. One day he was with Solange in the little red-lined lift which went up from the boutique to the studio, and she saw that he had been so preoccupied with his ideas that he had put on one black shoe and one brown! They both burst out laughing. Shortly afterwards, when they were celebrating St Catherine's day (November 25), he quite spontaneously gave her a lesson in dancing the samba. It was an unforgettable scene, but Balenciaga was full of humour and affection for those he liked.

After the war, the great fashion houses would organize foreign tours to promote their image. Balenciaga was not fond of these trips but he did agree in 1956 for his models to go to New York with Givenchy to show his latest creations to the New World. For Solange, it was a memorable occasion because Marlene Dietrich, a close personal friend of the couturier, came to meet them at the airport. Simple, warm and easy-going, she helped them to settle in, to get the dresses out of the trunks and even to iron them. Solange would never forget the magic moments she spent with the star: dinner at P J Clarke's, preparation for the show ... years later, when Marlene was giving a farewell at the Espace Cardin, Solange went to her dressing-room to embrace her and recall these wonderful moments in their past.

From time to time, Balenciaga agreed to allow Solange to pose for magazines wearing his creations. She greatly enjoyed the feverish atmosphere of the photo studio and particularly liked Carmel Snow and all the team from *Harper's Bazaar*. She also often appeared in French *Vogue* and *L'Officiel*. But to her mind all that really mattered was her work for Balenciaga. She admired his incredible perfectionism: he could make and undo a sleeve dozens of times in order to obtain the perfect shape. Moreover, he was one of the few couturiers who knew how to do everything. If need be, he could sew by hand or on a machine, cut his own cloth and was always willing to iron a few dresses himself. Only once did she ever think of leaving him, when Mistinguett asked her, every day for a whole month, to join her troupe as a dancer: 'Come on, you, with your pretty little legs, why don't you come with me?' But even Mistinguett's famous Parisian cheek couldn't persuade her.

In 1962, she decided to retire to devote more time to her twins, Danièle and Solange. Of course, she remained loyal to Balenciaga until his Parisian house closed* in 1968, attending his shows with the same pleasure, though she was now sitting with the audience. She was at last able to enjoy fully a spectacle that she had never previously seen.

---

* Like all Balenciaga's fans, Solange was devastated when she learned the news. She even wrote a poem to his unique style, signed 'Christange' (a contraction of her two first names).

Pierre Balmain

Pierre Balmain was one of the most refined couturiers of the 1950s and 1960s. Queen Sirikit, Marlene Dietrich, the Comtesse de Paris, Vivien Leigh, Jacqueline de Ribes, Cyd Charisse, Queen Marie-José of Italy, Brigitte Bardot: a balanced mixture of royalty, stars and society women hurried to his door to enjoy the privilege of wearing his clothes. A former assistant to Captain Molyneux and Lucien Lelong, and a native of Saint-Jean-de-Maurienne, he decided to open his own house in 1945, at No. 44, Rue François-Ier. His first collection was an instant success. He was the inventor of the *Jolie Madame* style, a delicate and sophisticated fashion intended solely for privileged society women. Pastel colours, precious furs and sumptuous embroidery were some features of the inimitable technique which contributed to his fame in the four corners of the world, recalled in his memoirs, *My Years and My Seasons*. Something else which contributed to his extraordinary success were his supermodels, among them Dan, Bronwen Pugh, Marie-Thérèse, Marine, Paulette and, most of all, the unforgettable Praline. Each was a muse who successively embodied his ideal of elegance to delight his public.

Pierre Balmain was also famous for his perfumes. *Elysée 64-83* (the telephone number of his fashion house) in 1946, *Vent Vert* in 1947, *Jolie Madame* in 1949, *Miss Balmain* in 1960 and, of course, *Ivoire* in 1979. When he died in 1982 Erik Mortensen, who had been his assistant since 1948, succeeded him until 1991, when a twenty-six-year old prodigy, Hervé Pierre, replaced him for three unforgettable collections. In January 1993, Oscar de La Renta took over as head of the haute couture department.

Marie-Thérèse

On February 5, 1951, Pierre Balmain presented his new Spring-Summer collection. The real event of the show was the appearance of Marie-Thérèse, the star model, in a mauve indoor outfit (corduroy trousers, with blouse and chiffon turban to match), accompanied by a poodle, wearing a diamond necklace, her hair dyed mauve for the occasion by the hairdresser Jean Clément. Some people applauded wildly, delighted by such eccentricity, while others described it as indecent and ridiculous. There was even a complaint from the Society for the Protection of Animals. Aside from the controversy, the event symbolized the vision of the 'Jolie Madame', which seemed to have come straight from a story by Jacques Chazot, as dreamed up by Pierre Balmain. The couturier entrusted this particular number, which so many models would have liked to display, to Marie-Thérèse — and not by chance.

The young woman had entered Balmain's in January 1950, after working for Madeleine de Rauch. The latter, whose house was at 27, Rue Jean-Goujon, was famous for her elegant, sporting style, ideal for members of the fashionable golf, riding or tennis clubs. Marie-Thérèse's beauty and style were certainly better suited to Balmain. A haughty blonde, she was the quintessential 'Parisienne'. Her charm, humour and her irresistible 'something' helped to make her one of the couturier's favourite models. Soon, with another ravishing blonde, Geneviève, she was joint favourite to succeed Praline in the much coveted role of chief model. As it happened, everyone was surprised by the striking resemblance between the designer's two new protégées. One day, as they were leaving a show in a top hotel in Denver, an American asked Marie-Thérèse: 'Are you twins?' Not understanding English, she smiled and said: 'No, French.'

For Balmain, she was the ideal person to embody 'Jolie Madame'. This heroine, whose style he would continue to perfect for some years, inspired his finest creations. There are many examples: one only has to think of the evening wear in the Spring-Summer collection of 1953, each item named after a famous château: Azay-le-Rideau, Beaugency, Laeken, Linderhof. Marie-Thérèse had an incomparable style when it came to showing off the ultra-formal evening wear that Balmain was especially fond of. At every show, the audience would hold its breath when she appeared. But Marie-Thérèse's work was not confined to posing and press shows. As well as working for Pierre Balmain, Marie-Thérèse was much in demand as a cover girl. She posed in the finest creations of all the great Parisian couturiers. Pierre Balmain himself always encouraged her to wear his designs for the fashion magazines. Here, too, she proved herself worthy of his confidence. She was photographed in the most characteristic creations of every new wave: a fur with an ocelot motif, entirely embroidered with sequins, for Philippe Pottier or Willy Rizzo in the Autumn of 1953; or in the afternoon suits which always delighted his clients, for Tom Kublin or Guy Arsac. The photographs have become classics.

To Balmain, she was far more than a supermodel, she was a faithful friend. He often invited her to 'Bon-Port', his house in Croissy, where she would meet his other regular guests, Marie-

Joseph d'Italie, the Jouhandeaus and Père Bernadet, a Savoyard priest. In Paris, she accompanied him to the theatre; in Milan they went to La Scala. From a professsional point of view, Balmain, who had every faith in her, would choose her to represent his house both in Paris and abroad. Thus, in 1954, he asked her to pose for the press in a coat of yellow Cheviot wool, created by Karl Lagerfeld, who had won the competition of the Syndicat de la Laine. The house of Balmain had made up the design which the young man had drawn. It was an historic occasion. And, in the many years she spent with Balmain, Marie-Thérèse also made several trips abroad. She went, for example, to South America in 1954 to promote a unique collection, made in Rhodiaceta cloth, which had been manufactured by Brazilian and French companies. Stopping over at Havana, Caracas, Rio, Buenos Aires, Lima and Santiago, Marie-Thérèse and her companions delighted the local press while visiting the archeological sites with Balmain, whose knowledge of the subject greatly impressed those around him. Then, there was the United States. In the summer of 1960, Marie-Thérèse scored a triumph on American television with 'Soir de Chambord', a strapless dress in sequinned tulle embroidered with pheasant feathers, which was the key creation in the new collection.

In 1962, she decided to leave the Rue François-Ier, since the work had not really left her any opportunity to develop her private life. She needed to make up for lost time. With her went the concept of the 'Jolie Madame' — and the golden age of the Balmain house. It had been a time when, if a client showed signs of excessive arrogance, they had made her try on every one of the clothes modelled by Marie-Thérèse — the slimmest model in Paris — while being watched by the assembled staff! It was a very 'haute couture' lesson in humility. In 1986, at the Pierre Balmain retrospective in the Palais Galliera, Marie-Thérèse agreed to take part in a film for German television, about her work with the late designer. In it, she recalled her early years, with feeling and humour: the misgivings of her provincial family, the luxury of the Balmain years and the development of fashion over two decades.

Praline

Aix-les-Bains, November 1947. Pierre Balmain is showing his very latest collection at the Splendide, one of the most elegant grand hotels in the spa. Janine, who will soon have been his star mannequin for ten months, triumphs every time she steps out on the catwalk. At the end of the show, when she appears in the bridal dress entirely embroidered with rosebuds, the audience is ecstatic. The young woman, more attractive than ever, looks like a delicious confection. Her baptism as a model was announced with a fanfare of publicity by the local press. She would soon leave behind the everyday round and all material considerations and choose a new first name; one that was poetic and evocative, symbolizing the dream evoked by haute couture throughout the world. This was how Simone Bodin and Germaine Lefèvre were to become, respectively, Bettina and

Capucine. Janine's name was already to hand: the pink and white bridal dress which she had worn with such delicate refinement made it inevitable. From then on she would be Praline. As with every baptism, there had to be a godfather and godmother. Major Larking and the Comtesse de Salverte were amused to take on the roles. Did they realize, as they participated in this apparently frivolous, empty ceremony, that they were present at the birth of a star who would become an emblematic figure for a whole generation?

At the end of 1947, Praline was far from being an unknown. After leaving Lelong, she had gone freelance for nearly eighteen months, before joining her friend Pierre Balmain, in February, as a supermodel. It was Tabard, a staff photographer at *Marie-Claire*, who had stopped her in the Place de l'Etoile in 1942 and advised her to take up modelling as a career. After successive rejections from Balenciaga, Schiaparelli and Bruyère, she finally joined Lelong. Thanks to Pierre Balmain and Christian Dior, at the time mere assistants, she had risen to become the star of the *cabine*. She recalls the two men admiringly in her memoirs, *Praline mannequin de Paris*: 'Imagine a starlet who was given work, for example, by [the film directors] Delannoy and Carné'.

Balmain was especially fond of seeing his designs shown off by her. Thus, despite the disapproval of Lelong, she had insisted on taking part in a show during the German Occupation wearing 'Petit Profit', a dress in black crêpe de Chine which had a considerable success, selling 360 copies. She had also aroused great interest by opening a show astride a bicycle to highlight one of his 'sporting' outfits. Their friendship contributed a good deal to the progress of the young couturier's career.

Praline was an offbeat and unpredictable personality. She could be irresistibly charming but also, at times, appear capricious and unbearable. On such occasions it was very hard to work with her. For example, panicking at the prospect of a new collection, she might vanish altogether a few hours before the show, and Ginette Spanier, the salon director, would have to set off in urgent search of her. She alone was able to track her down at Orly airport or in a railway station, on the point of leaving Paris. Even when she finally felt able to face the public eye, their difficulties were not necessarily over. Balmain always tried to define a theme, a sort of thread running through each new collection, and he would give his models a few instructions so that, while still preserving their own personalities, they could help him to suggest one or two central concepts. But Praline seemed utterly unable to accept any kind of advice. Immensely versatile, she would change her role with every new outfit she wore. Of course, the audience would look only at her, their fascination reinforced by the various rumours which used to circulate about her, for example that she would arrive for a fitting completely naked under her fur coat. One must try to imagine the effect of such stories — often true — in the climate of the 1940s.

However, her professionalism was undeniable, even though some interpreted it as pride inspired by jealousy. One day, two models came to the Rue François-Ier to offer their services to the couturier. They arrived in the middle of a fitting while Balmain was putting the finishing touches to an outfit on Praline, who was shivering with fever. She was suffering from the flu and obviously exhausted. The two young women expressed their astonishment at this unusual situation and, to their great surprise, were told simply that Praline would attend a fitting even if she were at death's door, because if she didn't, Balmain would be forced to use another model, and she would never stand for that! To calm the two new arrivals, who seemed to be terrified at the idea of catching Praline's flu, the couturier grabbed hold of a spray atomizer filled with *Vent Vert* and ordered them to open their mouths so that he could disinfect them. Once he had performed this piece of preventive medicine, he promptly went back to work. The anecdote is typical of the world of haute couture. However, Praline's refusal to give way to illness is very revealing. The title of supermodel has to be earned. She could always pretend to be on the point of vanishing on the eve of a big show, because she knew that she was essential to the success of the collection: the dresses had been built around her, to her size, and no one else could wear them. But she would never have missed a fitting session at the start of a collection, because in that case she would risk being put aside in favour of someone else in the couturier's imagination. At that stage, no one was irreplaceable, not even Praline, and she knew it.

Praline was equally famous in France and abroad. Her many trips with Pierre Balmain, and her work for designers like Fath, Rochas, Molyneux and Paquin (because she still continued to freelance), added to her fame. Wherever she went, she gave infinite care to refining her image; and she travelled all round the world, including Egypt and South Africa. Every appearance had to be unforgettable. So, in October and November 1950, the couturier and his model went to the United States to show off 180 designs typical of the Balmain house style. The centre-piece of the trip was an evening in New York, at the Waldorf Astoria, where Praline stepped out of a huge box carried by two servants, dressed in a magnificent evening gown. There was a burst of applause. She was equally successful in her tours of South America and throughout Europe.

At heart, she had what might familiarly be described as the mind of a shopgirl. She even claimed as much herself, comparing herself to a heroine from a novel by Delly and saying that this was largely due to her humble origins. She had been brought up in Le Bourget by her father, a bus driver, and her mother who worked in a glove factory. She used often to say that reading cinema magazines had helped her to overcome the hardships of everyday life when she was a teenager. She had to go out to work very early. At thirteen, after taking her school leaving certificate, she was successively an apprentice in a factory, a 'secretarial assistant', nursemaid, dressmaker and salesgirl. She married the actor Michel Marsay on February 5, 1947, and decided, in an acknowledgement of her childhood dreams, to take part in the 'Miss Cinémonde' competition, or-ganized by the magazine of that name. Pierre Balmain was irritated by the idea of his star model, the ambassador for one of the most elegant Parisian fashion houses, being associated with such a low-class event. He refused to lend her a dress for the final, and Praline consequently won the title — at the age of 24, in January 1948 — wearing a white satin sheath by Jacques Fath. The first prize was a trip to America, and espe-cially to Hollywood, and was considered to be a good starting-point for a film career. Before she left, Balmain (who had decided to make it up with her), gave a dinner in her honour at the Tour d'Argent and introduced her to Orson Welles. This meeting with one of the geniuses of the cinema gave her a foretaste of her stay in the movie capital of the world. As soon as she arrived, Praline, dressed by Germaine Lecomte, was warmly welcomed. There were press conferences, autograph signings and meetings with some of the most famous stars of the dream factory: Cary Grant, Charlie Chaplin, Joan Crawford and Shirley Temple. Of course, the title 'Miss *Cinémonde*' was no substitute for acting ability, so Praline decided to return to Paris and make her name as the best in her own field, which was that of a supermodel, rather than to stagnate as a second-rate actress in a country where she didn't even speak the language. Once back in France, she decided to go freelancing, while remaining the star of Balmain's shows. Her relationship with the couturier was always emotionally highly charged, involving violent arguments and almost hysterical reconciliations, which many people found exhausting. Knowing that they always attracted a crowd, they made sure that they frequently appeared in public together. They were rapturously applauded on June 30, 1948, in the Grande Nuit de Paris, held beneath the Eiffel Tower. The central event in the evening was a fashion show given by the leading Parisian couturiers, and the entrance of Praline, on the back of a pink elephant, was a triumph. It almost upstaged Rita Hayworth, who was also wearing Balmain, but, in her case, as a customer. However, their relationship was not just confined to such social occasions; there was a genuine friendship between them. In May the same year they went for a short holiday to Provence and were seen together at a bullfight in Nîmes; far from the photographers and from Parisian society, they shared moments of real intimacy. However, Balmain could never entirely forgive her 'infidelity'. From now on he would share out the best numbers in his new collections between several models. Praline, with a hint of bitterness and jealousy, once said of one of her rivals: 'My understudy has been tremendously successful! So much the better for me!'

In fact, her supremacy was never equalled. In the summer of 1951, she brought out her memoirs, *Praline mannequin de Paris*, written in a racy style, which became a bestseller. It demonstrated the extent of her popularity: never before had anyone in her profession published an autobiography.

In June 1953, the idyll was to end tragically. Praline died following an accident while at the wheel of her Citroën, on the road to Deauville. When he heard the news, Pierre Balmain rushed to her bedside, in the clinic at Neuilly, where she had been taken in a coma. She never regained consciousness. For the public, Praline was a heroine of the popular magazines that she loved — a sort of French version of the American Dream. Her funeral, at the Eglise Saint-Augustin, was splendid, the whole world of haute couture gathering to pay homage to the woman whom it saw as its most charming symbol.

Bronwen Pugh

The Balmain *cabine* was broadly divided into two main 'types'. On the one hand were the 'young girls', whose elegance was cheeky and impish: Marie-Thérèse, Geneviève, Sonia, Gigi and Paulette each filled the role in her own way. On the other, there were the 'women of the world', and in this, from the earliest days at Balmain, Dan and Jeanne Garat were the acknowledged leaders. The first, Baroness Danita Dangel, was the daughter of the former director of a Polish steel combine. Her Slavonic beauty was universally admired. Jeanne Garat, however, was much appreciated for her restrained, classical manner. She always looked back nostalgically to her time with Molyneux, where some of the models only showed the customers formal dresses. As for Bronwen Pugh, she undoubtedly also belonged to this second group. At Balmain's, she successfully embodied a style of faultless distinction, with a hint of austerity, but at the same time of nonchalance.

However, she was not universally welcomed on her arrival. At her first show, on a Sunday morning, for the staff and leading associates of the firm, she was greeted with an icy silence. Most of those present, starting with the couturier's mother, Madame Balmain, and Ginette Spanier, the salon director, thought that she would not fit. Only Balmain himself and Erik Mortensen were enthusiasts from the start, seeing her as the embodiment of an international refinement which would complement the typically Parisian 'Jolie Madame' style. Time was to prove them right. From her first 'press show', Bronwen's supreme grace elevated her to the rank of star. In his memoirs, Pierre Balmain recalls her decisive performance, when she appeared wearing 'a long evening dress, in a cloud of silk chiffon scarves printed with huge, dark flowers. The ensemble had been christened "Nemesis", and when Bronwen stepped forward proudly, her eyes fixed on the far distance and thoroughly determined to have her revenge on the doubters, she possessed a tragic beauty.'

The journalists, clients and buyers were fascinated, wondering who she could be. This magnificent and patrician beauty was of Welsh origin, the daughter of a judge, Lord Pugh. She had been, by turns, model and elocution teacher in London, before turning to British television. It was only after she gave up her career as a presenter on the small screen, after her first marriage ended, that she decided to apply to Balmain.

Ariane Tolokonnikoff, a former *chef de cabine*, recalls that Bronwen Pugh enjoyed a very special status. She would never take part in the endless fitting sessions which were the inevitable fate of all the girls in the house. She was also let off the daily three o'clock shows and the system by which models took it in turns to cover if a client arrived without prior arrangement. Instead, she would turn up a week before the collection for the final fittings, then show the creations to the press. Very tall and exceptionally slim, she would walk with long strides and a distant, abstracted air, without moving her arms, like a living statue. Her dark hair and huge blue eyes, totally ignoring everything that was going on around her, her milk-white skin, her haughty and condescending attitude: all these invariably made a strong impression on the audience. Eugenia Sheppard, something of an institution at the *New York Herald Tribune*, humorously described her at one show, 'dragging her fur coat behind her, as if she had just killed it and was bringing it back to her partner.'

She couldn't fail. Before entering the salon, Bronwen had a habit of slightly disarranging her hair to give herself a subtly untidy look. This derived from a concept of elegance typical of the style of the British aristocracy, which has an aversion for the way the *nouveaux riches* always imagine that a flawless appearance is distinguished. For Bronwen, Balmain made long tubular dresses, without décolleté, often accompanied by simple cardigans with an impeccable line. She was quite spectacular in furs for evening wear, very austere, their severity modified by some delicate embroidery. The creation, 'Grande Duchesse', a sheath of fine violet satin of timeless purity, in which she posed for Tom Kublin in the Autumn of 1957, perfectly illustrated the sort of outfit that she would show. The picture is particularly noteworthy, since Bronwen was not often photographed. Her unusual and angular style was too personal, and offered little with which the readers of women's magazines could identify. Only a few artists like Helmut Newton (whose enduring quest for anything unusual or eccentric always made him tend towards off-beat beauties) asked her to work for them. Some years later, in Norman Parkinson's *Lifework*, Newton admitted that, taking the 1950s as a whole, his favourite models were (in order of preference), Bronwen Pugh, Margaret Hibble and Maggie Tabberer.

When Pierre Balmain wanted to transform a show into a 'happening', he always turned to Bronwen first of all. So, one day, François André asked the couturier to take part in a July 14 gala at the 'Ambassadeurs' in Deauville. At that time of the year, it was both too early to show any of the new models and too late to exhibit the dresses from the previous collection, which had been so often photographed in the magazines. How could he satisfy a cynical and sophisticated audience? Balmain selected just three dresses: one blue, the second white and the third red, in homage to the French flag. Then he asked Van Cleef and Arpels to get together all their sapphires, rubies and diamonds, making an ideal decoration for each model in the appropriate colour. At the end of the show, four servants from the casino brought a giant jewel box onto the stage. Bronwen, wearing a white satin fur, was entirely covered with stone-encrusted diamonds, in every imaginable form: diamond rivières, bracelets, earrings, rings and brooches. As motionless and impassive as a Greek statue, she attracted every eye. Only a hint of an ironic smile, mocking such deliberate ostentation, suggested a trace of life. In honour of the most precious of tricolour flags, the band struck up La Marseillaise, and a firework display began to erupt above the gardens. It is impossible to imagine a more theatrical effect.

Bronwen Pugh was a model at Pierre Balmain's until her marriage to Lord Astor, whom she had met at St Moritz when she went there to display the latest collection at a special evening show. Later, she could still be seen in the salons at Rue François-Ier, as a loyal client. When her husband died, Lady Astor retired from all social life and decided to devote all her energies to a centre for the destitute in Surrey.

Pierre Cardin

Pierre Cardin had a fairytale debut in the world of haute couture. In 1945, at the age of twenty-three, he joined Paquin's and helped to make the magnificent costumes for *La Belle et la Bête*, the cult film by Jean Cocteau. Already, between 1900 and 1920, the house of Paquin had shown an affinity with the theatre, when it had worked with Léon Bakst. But the costumes for Josette Day and Jean Marais, designed by Christian Bérard as a tribute to Gustave Doré, were a masterly example of collaboration between a great couturier and a film director. There is no doubt that they helped to influence Pierre Cardin's quest for perfection. After a period at Schiaparelli's, he chose to spend some time concentrating on cinema and theatre, mainly for Cocteau. Finally, yielding to the attraction of haute couture, which was such a lively field in that period after the war, he joined Dior where he saw the creation of the 'flower women' of the New Look. The technical details of the dresses completed an education which he had begun with a tailor in St Etienne at the age of fourteen, and continued through years of experiment. In 1951, he felt confident enough to set up his own house at 10, Rue Richepance. His first collection only included day wear, and its elegant simplicity aroused a great deal of enthusiasm. Helped by this early success, he was able in 1953 to move to 82, Faubourg St Honoré. The most prominent women wore his dresses, which were very highly tailored and pure in line. Indeed, some of his customers became valued and even indispensible assistants, like Nicole Alphand and Princess Odile de Croÿ.

Cardin soon became known for his feeling for the unusual. With his discovery of Hiroko Matsumoto in 1957 during a trip to Japan, he played a pioneering role by featuring an Asian supermodel. Among his other innovations, we might also mention a revolutionary line for men in 1958 and a fruitful cooperation with department stores in the 1960s, as well as the popularizing of the unisex fashion and of designer ready-to-wear at a reasonable price. Cardin, a man of broad culture, was continually trying new things.

His empire includes a perfume department (*Suite 16, Cardin, Choc* and *Rose de Cardin* are among its scents), and various lines of accessories — fashion, interior design, and so on. In 1971, he transformed the Théâtre des Ambassadeurs into the 'Espace Cardin', a specially designed space in which Marlene Dietrich chose to take her farewell from the stage. A short time later, he bought the restaurant Maxim's, where he gave dinners blending artists and opinion formers into a harmonious cocktail. Finally, in 1992, he succeeded Pierre Dux beneath the famous dome of the French Academy — yet another first, since never before had a couturier been granted the exceptional honour of being made a member.

Hiroko Matsumoto

In June 1957, Pierre Cardin arrived in Tokyo on the inaugural flight of Air France's transpolar route, Paris-Hamburg-Tokyo. No Parisian couturier had previously been invited to Japan to demonstrate his creative talent. It was love at first sight between the Japanese and the young Frenchman. On this trip, crucial for his career, he met Hiroko Matsumoto, already a supermodel in her own country, after selecting her to work with him when seeing the photographs of the eighty most beautiful Japanese women. She was waiting for him at the airport, in a ceremonial kimono, offering the traditional welcoming bouquet of flowers. For twenty-seven days and in sixteen lecture/demonstrations, she showed the artist's creations to the élite of the Japanese fashion world, together with Hélène Delrieu, the model who had accompanied Cardin on his journey. At the end of his stay,

Cardin had only one thought, which was to bring Hiroko to France and to make her the star of his *cabine*. As a well-mannered girl from a good family (which, in her country, implied a high level of discipline), she thought for a long time before accepting. It was more than three years, but when she did take the plunge, she transformed herself, as she herself said, jokingly, 'into the first Japanese export product, well ahead of Sony and Toyota.'

Hiroko stepped onto French soil on July 15, 1960, to show the new Autumn-Winter collection. She can still rememeber the air of mystery surrounding the Cardin salons, as elsewhere, at that time. The great couturiers were so afraid of 'spies' who would stick at nothing to steal their ideas, that they worked behind closed shutters, even demanding that, between fittings, their models should wear long dustsheets, coloured green at Cardin's and tied at the neck, so that no one could glimpse the designs before they were shown to the press. From then, until she settled finally in Paris in 1963, she constantly flew backwards and forwards between France and Japan.

Thanks to Hiroko, Cardin invented a new idea of femininity and distinction at the heart of Parisian haute couture. Small, her features as finely modelled as a Tanagra figurine, she brought a note of Asiatic restraint and fragility into the theatrical world of European and American elegance. Modest, withdrawn, she was the complete antithesis of the versatile divas represented by Praline or Ivy Nicholson. In front of the camera, Hiroko never smiled, which gave her beauty a sophistication full of melancholy. Her expression was impenetrable, and she did not need to use lipstick. Only her eyes, made up to accentuate their natural shape, and her hair stood out in photographs: for the latter, Maria Carita recreated for her the famous Louise Brooks bob. As for her shows, everyone who was anyone in Paris hurried to see them: Jeanne Moreau, Marcel Achard, Annabel and Bernard Buffet, Claude Pompidou, Jacqueline Delubac, Hélène Lazareff. . . the list is endless. All were fascinated by her fine bone structure, her slow, soft, delicate gestures, and the lightness of her walk. For Hiroko, Pierre Cardin devised a fashion with pure and fluid lines: a lot of tuberoses made from brightly-coloured crêpe and silks, with sometimes a hint of precious fur or a fringe of rare feathers for ornament. She also inspired his first daring transparencies, like the evening dress composed of a long skirt in a lovely deep yellow shade, belted in black grosgrain, and a mini-cape in flimsy chiffon worn next to the skin. His clients rushed to buy the dresses he made for her. In seven years with Cardin, Hiroko showed fourteen wedding dresses, the undoubted stamp of the star model. At the same time she was much in demand for the most prestigious magazines, starting with *Vogue.* Photographed by Irving Penn, Richard Avedon, Jeanloup Sieff, John French or Yoshi Takata, she naturally symbolized the perfect Cardin woman, but she also posed in clothes by Givenchy and Balenciaga. Hiroko still remembers the luxurious world that surrounded these great American photographers. The team from *Harper's Bazaar* often worked at night and magnificent buffets were set up so that everyone there could eat or drink at any time. Alexandre himself did Hiroko's hair during these sessions, since *Harper's* always demanded the best and most eminent practitioners in any field. In such circumstances, life seemed very easy. . .

However, in 1967, she gave up her career without any regrets, to devote herself to bringing up her daughter, Olivia, the child of her marriage with Henry Berghauer, whom she had met at Cardin's. One of the most fêted debutantes in Paris, Olivia now works for the couturier Valentino in Rome. Because of her friendship with François Truffaut, Hiroko did agree to play the part of a Japanese woman with whom Antoine Doinel falls in love in *Domicile conjugal* (1970). At first, Truffaut had asked her to find a Japanese actress able to play opposite Jean-Pierre Léaud. When none of the candidates seemed to correspond to the type he was looking for, he gradually came to consider Hiroko herself for the lead. Since she had never acted before, she refused at first, but eventually, on Truffaut's insistence, agreed, as long as he changed the script. In the original version, it was Antoine who breaks off the relationship with the Asian woman, but Hiroko had no intention of being rejected on the screen. Amused by this request, Truffaut was quite happy to make his hero the abandoned lover. The film was a great success and remains one of the most accomplished of Truffaut's Antoine Doinel series. But Hiroko did not feel that she had the makings of an actress and never tried to become one. Now married to Jean-Claude Cathalan, she has for some years been in charge of French *Vogue*'s Japanese office, while remaining a central figure in Parisian society and cultural life.

Gabrielle Chanel

George Bernard Shaw considered her the most important woman of the century, together with Marie Curie; and Gabrielle Chanel is undoubtedly the best-known figure in the realm of fashion. Her life reads like a novel — and has, indeed, been adapted several times for the stage and the screen. Katharine Hepburn played her on the Broadway stage and Marie-France Pisier on film. She has also been the subject of numerous books and documentaries.

It was Gabrielle Chanel who succeeded, in the years between the wars, in responding to a real desire for emancipation among the women of the time. The 'Chanel Girl' is at once independent, sporty and elegant. Much to her delight, right up to the time of her death, in January 1971, her inimitable designs (which were constantly copied, nonetheless) profoundly transformed the lives of women throughout the world. They represent a huge step forward in the history of women's fashion. After her death, she was succeeded as head of Chanel by Gaston Berthelot, Ramon Esparza, Jean and Yvonne, former assistants of 'Mademoiselle'; by Philippe Guibourgé and finally, from 1983 onwards, by Karl Lagerfeld.

Beginning in 1911, Chanel specialized in making hats, first in Compiègne, then in premises on the Boulevard Malesherbes, before finally opening her own shop in Deauville in 1913.

During the First World War, she had to leave Normandy for Biarritz, where she dressed all the high-class refugees. Finally, in 1919, she founded her Parisian house in Rue Cambon, only however settling at No. 31 in that street in 1928. However, it was from 1919 onward that Chanel revolutionized Parisian haute couture by bringing in what her friend Paul Morand called: 'Poverty for millionaires': the first little black dresses, at a time when black was for funerals and servants, recalling the orphan's uniform that she wore as a child, short hair, suntanned skin and scents which achieved refinement through restraint — the famous *No 5* in 1921, then *Gardénia, Bois des îles, Cuir de Russie, No. 22* and finally *No 19* in 1970, just before her death. Her amazingly simple tubular evening dresses permitted women to dress themselves, without the help of a chambermaid: no more flounces, frills or corsets, but supple, 'epidermic' materials like jersey, costume jewellery — designed by artists as different as Fulco di Verdura and Paul Iribe — and borrowings from the masculine wardrobe, such as jockey sweaters, sailor trousers, boaters and Austrian hunting jackets trimmed discreetly . . . the line was at once fluid, tapered and immediately identifiable.

In 1939, she had to shut down her fashion house. The war saw the end of the 1930s, a golden age for cultural life in Paris. Chanel had been one of the most sought after members of Parisian society between the wars: Diaghilev, Misia Sert, Cocteau, Bérard, Dali, Marlene Dietrich, Picasso, Stravinsky, Reverdy and Visconti were all among her closest friends.

Fifteen years later, however, in February 1954, at the age of seventy-one, Chanel decided to show a new collection as a reaction to the designs of Dior and Balmain, which, in her eyes, by reviving half-cup bras, basques and petticoats, were uncomfortable in every way — and both couturiers worked for a privileged clientele, while Chanel wanted universal appeal. At first, the French press was sceptical, or even insulting about a style which it considered backward-looking, but the Americans exhibited a high degree of enthusiasm. Thanks to their wholehearted support, Chanel was able in record time to recover the high status she had enjoyed before the war. From now on, women would rush to buy her famous tweed suits, the equivalent of the man's suit, which by a miracle of balance had become the height of elegance and femininity. 'Everything is in the proportions,' Chanel used to say. 'The proportions of the head to the bust, and the legs to the whole.'. Hers was a golden rule. The magic of these light suits, with no underwiring, was a matter of architecture. The precision of the armholes made for graceful shoulders, while the skirts, held at the point of the hips, allowed the wearer to walk naturally. A slender bust, long, fine legs and arms, and a low neckline: the style itself was unchanging, with only the details altered to give the illusion of a different woman: a colour, a pattern, a piece of braid or a jewelled button. And, finally, the other major constituent of her success: her models, the thoroughbreds of the breed. There were Marie-Hélène Arnaud and Susy Parker, of course, but also her 'women of the world': Odile de Croÿ, Mimi d'Arcangues, Paule Rizzo, Guylaine Arsac, Shawn Trabber, Gisèle Franchomme, Claude de Leusse and Paule de Mérindol, to name but a few.

Mimi d'Arcangues

While Odile de Croÿ, Gisèle Francohomme, Paule Rizzo and Claude de Leusse, each in her own way, interpreted a version of the typical 'Parisienne' as seen by Chanel, 'Mademoiselle' saw Mimi d'Arcangues as a perfect vision of cosmopolitan elegance. Everything fitted her for this role. Eugenia-Maria de Ouro Prêto, affectionately nicknamed 'Mimi', was the great-granddaughter of one of the founders of Brazil and was born in Vienna while her father, an ambassador, was serving there. She was brought up successively in Chile, Turkey and France, where she arrived in the early 1950s, at the age of fifteen, to continue her education. Equally fluent in Portuguese, English, French and Spanish, she always seemed ready to set off for a new climate — a 'Chanel Girl', citizen of the world, whose greatest talent was undeniably her hunger for life. Fairy, clown or bird of paradise, she was able to appreciate every moment of her time on earth with an intense appetite.

In 1953, at a *feria* in Seville, Guy d'Arcangues, one of the most eligible batchelors of his generation, noticed in the middle of the crowd a young woman riding a white horse and dressed in Andalucian costume. Enchanted by this vision, he wanted to make her acquaintance immediately, but she had already vanished. Was she a dream? Refusing to be discouraged, he hunted for her all day through the town. That evening, sad and dejected, he met some friends on a boat. Of course, the mysterious Amazon was one of the guests. The story may sound like a badly-written romance, but this is really how Guy and Mimi d'Arcangues met. Inseparable from that moment on, they were married in April 1955. A year later, their only son, Michel, was born.

At the time when he married Mimi, Guy d'Arcangues was a typical man of the world, handsome, refined and attractive. His presence at a dinner or a party (he was always to be seen in the major social events of the early 1950s), guaranteed the success of the occasion. For the record, we can mention the costumed ball, 'Les Fêtes Galantes', given at Biarritz in 1953 by the Marquis de Cuevas. Guy d'Arcangues appeared as a Martinique planter of the 18th Century, while the Duchess of Argyll was dressed as an angel — wings and all — and Merle Oberon as a rococo version of a Greek nymph. It seemed inevitable that he would appeal to Mimi, who very much liked to enjoy herself. However, behind the façade of the cultured aristocrat, she also perceived in him a genuine desire to become a writer, and encouraged her husband's literary vocation, even helping him to translate and adapt a novel by the Spanish writer, Enrique Meneses, which appeared in the year of their marriage, 1955, under the title: *Frappe mais écoute*. As a tribute to their love for one another, Guy d'Arcangues wrote *Eugenia*, a collection of poems entirely dedicated to her, which was published in 1958.

That same year, on the advice of Paule Rizzo who was herself a model at Chanel's, Mimi joined the *cabine* of 'women of the world' in the Rue Cambon. 'Mademoiselle' immediately appreciated her exuberant beauty, her ironic smile and her pleasure in life itself. Tall, slender and dark, Mimi was able to make whatever she was wearing look elegant, without the least affectation. When she first arrived at Chanel's, the magazine *Jours de France* devoted several pages to a feature on her, illustrating the different phases of her first day's work: a course in make-up and haircare with Marie-Hélène Arnaud, learning the famous Chanel style of walking, depicting a show for clients in the salon, and finally a dinner at Maxim's given by her husband to mark the occasion. Mimi admired the freedom of movement offered by the Chanel style. The dresses lived with the body, the legs were outlined under the tweed of the suits, and the chiffons of the evening outfits revealed a slender and graceful figure. Of all the shows in which she took part, that for the Spring-Summer collection in 1959 must certainly remain the most successful. Every time she stepped out on the catwalk, she was greeted with admiration by an audience that was notoriously blasé and hard to please. Chanel had undoubtedly surpassed herself, from the suits — narrow at the waist and slightly tipped from front to back — to the Chinese-inspired tunics, perfect for a cocktail party. There was also a sheath, with a straight, bright yellow brocade coat, lined in purple velvet and hemmed in sable; and the suit in coarse white, green and beige *pied-de-coq*, worn with a blouse in lime green shantung, with no accessories except gilt chains and Byzantine crosses. For Mimi, 'Mademoiselle' especially designed the first abstract prints, such as the beige and grey suit, its jacket lined in the same material as the blouse with a geometrical motif in shades of cream, black and nut-brown. Shortly afterwards, every elegant woman looked like a painting by Mondrian.

Wherever she was in the world, Mimi had friends. Her ability to listen and her immediate understanding of the most delicate situation made her irresistible to everybody. After just a few minutes, a complete stranger could feel magically transported into the presence of a close confidante. Where friendship was concerned, Mimi had no sense of age or frontier. As soon as she arrived in Rio, she would meet up with her oldest companions and feel that she had never left them: Vinicius de Moraes, who was at the same time a diplomat, a poet and a musician; the singer Joao Gilberto; the guitarist Baden Powell; the composer Antonio Carlos Jobim; the writer Ruben Braga; and the painter Caribê, for whom she had posed in her teens. They were the cultural élite of the country. She always came back from Brazil in a state of euphoria, light and golden — a thoroughly rejuvenating experience, a health cure of sea, sunlight and bossa nova. In Paris, her close friends made up a similarly eclectic group: Roger Vadim, who gave her a part in *Les Liaisons dangereuses*; Jean Babilée; Boris Vian; Lilou Marquand; and Claude de Leusse — 'her sister', in the words of Michel d'Arcangues. Mimi would take them to Castel and Régine's, where they would spend hours trying out all the new dances. She slept very little, travelled ceaselessly, went out every evening and smoked a great deal. One day, at dawn, she decided to borrow a friend's car to get home. Driving along the quais she suddenly found herself, without quite knowing how, thrown into the middle of the Seine, where she had to swim to safety in her Chanel evening dress. A shocked sailor pulled her out and she spent three days in an expensive clinic. Having emerged from the adventure without a scratch, she spent her time there receiving her friends. She was irrepressible.

Only illness could defeat such energy. Tired and weak, Mimi decided to settle finally in Arcangues, the marvellous estate near Biarritz which she enjoyed so much. Bit by bit, she cut herself off from the world, to spare her friends the sight of her suffering. Closer than ever to her husband and her son, she shared with them alone these precious moments of intimacy in which laughter took the place of tears. However, on September 15, 1991, exhausted, she lost the battle, leaving a void in the hearts of all those who loved her which nothing could ever fill.

Marie-Hélène Arnaud

In 1954, Gabrielle Chanel decided to reopen her fashion house after an absence of sixteen years, adapting the basic principles of her refined and timeless style of elegance to life in the 1950s. This was when she hired as one of her models a young woman, Marie-Hélène Arnaud, who had just taken her baccalauréat in philosophy and arrived at Rue Cambon one day with her father, hoping to work for 'Mademoiselle'. Miraculously, she was the living incarnation of the feminine ideal so dear to Chanel. Beautiful without being aggressive, refined but not ostentatious, she had an innate sense of how to wear the famous suits and the magical evening dresses, becoming known around the world as 'The Chanel Girl'. She soon became the designer's favourite model, her constant inspiration.

At the time of the collections, her dresses were always the first to go, because the clients were fascinated by her bearing. Marie-Hélène was a younger, irresistible double of the great 'Mademoiselle' herself: she had copied her gestures and her casual manner of playing with her cigarette or tying her mink by both sleeves around her neck. When she was on the catwalk, with a white camellia in her auburn hair, the audience was delighted by her famous 'Chanel' pose: one foot forward, flat belly, head held high, chin up and one hand in the pocket of her skirt. For her, Chanel brought freshness and colour to her shows, transforming Rue Cambon into the world headquarters of youthful elegance. On Marie-Hélène, the mossy tweeds of the Chanel suits, with their blurred tones were transformed into hints of oats, caviar, candy pink, Virginia tobacco, apricot sorbet or heather, their luminosity recalling the Scottish highlands.

There can be no doubt that Marie-Hélène was stifled by this relationship in which she played Galatea to Gabrielle Chanel's Pygmalion which meant that she only existed through 'Mademoiselle'. She left for a while to become a cover girl and at the same time the house star of Guy Laroche. She appeared on many magazine covers and posed for the élite of international fashion photographers. But she could not long resist the call of Rue Cambon and came back less than two years later, both as an assistant and as star model. She was always the one to wear dress or suit No. 5, the designer's 'lucky number' marked in red on a white wooden rectangle, which would open the show. She also acted as part public relations officer and part dragon on the gate, forming a protective shield around Chanel and sifting any request to see her. Yet, face-to-face with 'Mademoiselle' in person, she was sweet and self-effacing, never uttering a word of contradiction. In general, she spoke little and remained very withdrawn — quite unlike the other models of the house, who were women of the world exercising a dazzling and sometimes cruel wit — like piranhas in furs. Marie-Hélène was apparently only a little more at ease in her love life. The press made a great fuss about her affair with Robert Hossein, whom she met when he was filming *Le Jeu de la vérité*, but the young woman's enduring doubt, and self-doubt, were to undermine what seemed a promising relationship, shortly before the magnificent engagement party which Chanel had wanted to throw for her protégée. In fact, the only real love of her life was her father, whom she even brought to work in the Rue Cambon. When he had to leave, she could not bring herself to continue there without him. Even though Chanel, for whom she was a replacement for husband, child and family, begged her to stay, she steadfastly refused to do so.

At the start of the 1960s, she created her own lines, under the auspices of the Grande Maison de Blanc, in the Place de l'Opéra. She made her debut in 1962 with five seamstresses, transforming her apartment in the Rue Michel-Ange into a fashion house. But the new venture was never to prove a success. Like many models, she also tried to make a career in the cinema. She had had a bit part in 1959, in *Gigi*, the elegant musical comedy directed by Vincente Minnelli from the novel by Colette. In a very brief scene set in Maxim's, the twenty-three-year old Marie-Hélène made a spectacular entrance on the arm of Maurice Chevalier, wearing an evening dress designed by Cecil Beaton. Alas, her film career was confined to walk-on parts which were certainly radiant but without dialogue and always utterly forgettable. Those who are curious about such things may also remember her fleeting appearance in 1964 in one of André Hunebelle's *Fantomas* films, where she gave a somewhat unconvincing performance as a mysterious, silent lady. Once more, she did not speak a word throughout the film, playing opposite Jean Marais and Mylène Demongeot whose humour and vitality only served to emphasize her lack of professional skill. Enough of cinema — Marie-Hélène soon realized that it was not so easy to stand on her own two feet, especially after years of a privileged existence with Chanel. She worked in succession for the French Tourist Authority and in an art gallery, never managing to recapture the glamour of her career as a supermodel but having to face up to the tragic fate of women who have been magnificent and adored but who grow old alone. She was found dead in her bath one morning in October 1986. Was it suicide or a simple heart attack? No one will ever know, and the facts are not important. Just remember her luminous beauty in the film *Mannequins de Paris*: a self-contained young woman, deeply wounded, who remains for ever the ideal ambassador for the Chanel style around the world.

Christian Dior

In 1949, a mere two years after he had opened his fashion house, a Gallup Poll was already showing Christian Dior to be one of the four best-known names in the world, alongside Stalin, Gandhi and Chaplin. But his career was very short, barely ten years from 1947 to the year of his death, 1957, after which he was succeeded as head of the House of Dior by Yves Saint Laurent, Marc Bohan and Gianfranco Ferré.

He started late in life — he was forty-two in 1947 — yet this was to prove crucial in the history of women's clothes. The industrialist Marcel Boussac could hardly have guessed that, by putting his trust in this unknown, he would be taking part in one of the most fascinating episodes in the history of Parisian haute couture. The Dior empire was soon to be divided into several departments, each of which enjoyed dramatic success: haute couture, boutique lines, accessories and such perfumes as *Miss Dior* in 1947, then *Diorama* and *Diorissimo*

Dior's first collection, the legendary New Look, shown on February 12, 1947, at 30, Avenue Montaigne, was an instant triumph. Soft, rounded shoulders, emphasis on bust and hips, wasp waist and a skirt like a corolla covering the calf: a flower woman. Such refinement had not been seen since before the wartime years of austerity, when the watchwords were rationing and utility. Inevitably, when they witnessed such a prodigal use of materials, some people said it was indecent. For 'Chérie', an afternoon dress, he used 200 metres of faille, but he beat even this record with 'Amérique', an evening dress which took 300 metres of pink and white tulle. Even *Vogue* christened the new line 'Haute Couture's Battle of the Marne'. Despite this, in the same year, the couturier was awarded the Fashion Oscar by the Dallas firm of Nieman Marcus.

The great strength of Christian Dior was not giving way to the easy temptation to sacrifice everything to create merely a graceful appearance. From the first collection to the last (the 'spindle' — *fuseau* — line), his workshops would patiently construct each dress with the same degree of attention. His second major quality was also knowing how to respond to those who wanted something unusual at every show as well as the majority of women whose taste was much more conservative. Thus, he would always display a small number of highlighted designs which were very spectacular and representative of the new line, while offering modified versions of the same dresses, undoubtedly more wearable, which obviously made up the main part of his collections. Who were his clients? They included the Duchess of Windsor, Lady Marriott (who would order no less than forty items a season), Madame Martinez de Hoz, Princess Margaret and Marlene Dietrich, all loyal supporters from the start. Women really did play a decisive role in the couturier's life — from his indispensible assistants, Mitza Bricard, Raymonde Zehnacker and Marguerite Carré, to all his models, the most famous in Paris, whom he called 'the girls', 'the fairies' and 'my advocates'. The magic of the Dior shows owes much to Alla, Lucky, Sylvie, France, Victoire, Lia, Tania, Claire and Angèle.

At his funeral, in the Eglise Saint-Honoré-d'Eylau, hundreds of people, colleagues, clients and simple members of the public, came to pay their last respects. In the nave, draped in black, the coffin was decked with the couturier's favourite flower, lily of the valley, and the congregation could hear music specially composed by his friend Henri Sauguet. As they stood there, sad and meditative, all might have recalled those few lines from his second volume of memoirs, *Dior by Dior*: 'I think it was Alphonse Daudet who once wrote that he would like to become a merchant of happiness through his works; in my modest role as a couturier, I am pursuing the same goal.'

He accomplished his mission.

The Period of Christian Dior and Yves Saint Laurent

Alla

In the late 1950s, the world of Parisian haute couture, although very conservative, developed a liking for Asian models. In 1957, Pierre Cardin discovered Hiroko Matsumoto, then shortly afterwards, Mom Srey Neam, a ravishing nineteen-year old Cambodian beauty. Other couturiers quickly followed suit. Yves Saint Laurent took on Fidélia, a tremendously chic Eurasian, and Guy Laroche turned to Anne, a young woman from Hong Kong. The Japanese girl Katsuko Matsuda and the Chinese Moee Yip were soon taking part in their first shows, for Louis Féraud and Antonio del Castillo respectively, at Lanvin's. We might also mention Seignon, a beauty of mixed Scottish and Burmese origin and the darling of the fashion world on both sides of the Channel. Asian models were equally popular in the field of international fashion photography, where Richard

Avedon introduced the splendid China Machado in 1959, a half-Portuguese, half-Thai woman, who had for a time been the star at Givenchy. In the second half of the following decade this vitally important trend was to give the green light to the arrival of the first great black models, including Donyale Luna, Naomi Sims and Beverley Johnson. However, it was Christian Dior who opened the way in 1947 by using an Asian model. He hired Alla, whose mother was Russian and father Manchu, once more demonstrating the extent of his good sense in the matter, despite all the controversy that it aroused.

Alla turned up at Dior's a short while after he had shown his very first collection, and everyone was talking about the 'New Look'. In fact, she was accompanying a friend who hoped to be taken on as a replacement model. Ironically, Alla was chosen instead of her friend. What had she been doing up to this moment which was to have such a decisive effect on her life? According to some, she was a dancer at the Lido, while others say she was an interpreter. Which is correct? The second seems the most likely hypothesis, since, as Christian Dior said of her in his second volume of memoirs, 'Alla speaks all languages without an accent, as if she had been cradled simultaneously in all parts of the world.'

In any event, the young woman made a great impression on the designer. He recalls the meeting in a lively passage from *Dior by Dior*: 'Enigmatic and always a little mysterious, a model must "grab" you. The theatrical expression, "to have a stage presence", while often a cliché, takes on its full sense here. It was because of her presence that I hired Alla.' And: 'she is a natural born model. From one day to the next, we made her show a whole collection. She walked through it with that impassive and distant air, through which she can still demonstrate all her Slavonic spontaneity.'

Some of the designer's colleagues and assistants were not slow to react with surprise and incomprehension: how could he use an Asian model to show outfits intended for Western clients? For Dior, who had no intention of gratuitously provoking controversy, the answer was clear: 'While Alla's face has all the mysterious charm of the East, she is still half Russian. As a result she has a perfectly European body and I know that any woman who chooses a design she has worn will not be disappointed'.

Christian Dior was unfailingly courteous but his sense of hierarchy was immoveable. Nothing must upset the very exact order that existed within his salons. Moreoever, he had little personal contact with his professional entourage, and his colleagues did not know the man behind the great couturier. Nonetheless, every member of the staff — from a seamstress in the workshops to the person in charge of the press service — could have access to him to express their complaints and anxieties. The same was also true, of course, of his 'girls'. Indeed, the model's opinion was crucial as long as it respected the unity and meaning of his work. In *Dior by Dior*, he recalls the last stage in preparation of a new collection, when he had to dispense with a few creations he considered less interesting than the rest, a choice which was essential if the overall quality was to be maintained: 'On such occasions, some tears were unavoidable. Alla, usually impassive and unemotional, puts on a tragic performance in my office. She doesn't have to speak; a single glance of her half-Salv, half-Manchu eyes tells me everything.

"So, do you want that dress of yours?"

"Oh, yes, Monsieur! It's one of the best . . ."

"But Alla, don't you think it's very like the suit you wore at the time of the last collection?"

"Ah, Monsieur, I'm sure it will be a success."

Then, after all, isn't she my first audience? She's a woman, she likes dresses and — it does help — she knows her stuff. Already, I'm three-quarters won round. And when Alla comes back, wearing the condemned dress, I have to give in.'

Dior's confidence in Alla was shown by the number and quality of her different appearances in a press show. Take, for example, the show for the Autumn-Winter collection in 1949–50 in which she showed sixteen of the most prestigious creations: 'Barnabé', 'Campagnole', 'Intrigue', 'Cap Horn' and 'Décision' in the morning; 'Pattes de Velours', 'Jeu de Société', 'Balthazar' and 'Labyrinthe' in the afternoon; and finally, in the evening, the most spectacular ensembles, 'Beau Ténébreux', 'Monseigneur', 'Melchior', 'Derain', 'Nocturne', 'Vie en Rose' and, above all, 'Junon', the key piece in the show, a gala dress in blue tulle, with a skirt formed of petals embroidered with blue-green sequins. As far as Dior was concerned, Alla was a talented model because she could wear everything. From the 'Tulipe' line (characterized by the expansion of the bust and the obliteration of the hips) to the 'H-line', or 'Haricot Vert' (based on prolonging and thinning the bust, in order to make the body look more slender), she was always in harmony with his vision of the ideal woman, as it varied from one season to the next. Moreover, Alla was one of the few to meet with unanimous approval from her fellow-models: 'a queen' according to Victoire Doutreleau; 'the star of stars, impossible to equal' according to Denise Sarrault; 'a piece of Ming porcelain, dark and lanky' to Freddy, she was for Viviane Porte-Deblème an unforgettable vision'; and for Praline, 'a charming Indochinese, slender as a creeper'. The model Lucky called her 'a rare plant . . . an Oriental goddess'. Jean Dawnay, in *Model Girl*, speaks of, 'Alla, the lovely Chinese model, with her pirouetting walk and her cool serenity in the dressing room when everyone else was shrieking and pushing'. This wave of superlatives was quite exceptional in a world where ferocious competition was a part of the profession. Alla became so famous that she was often requested for press shows or gala evenings by other famous fashion houses, like Biki and Schubert in Italy, as well as for advertisements by the major cosmetic films, like Chen Yu.

Alla posed for a lot of illustrators and photographers, from Louise Dahl-Wolfe to Harry Meerson, not forgetting Richard Avedon and Willy Maywald. Avedon did some superb photographs of her at the casino in Le Touquet in August 1954, together with the great cover girl Sunny Harnett. Maywald, however, was better than anyone at enhancing her haughty and distant beauty. There is, for example, the photograph, taken in 1948, in which she is wearing an Emba mutation mink coat; the first perfect white mink.

Travel was also part of Alla's work as an ambassador for the firm. In general, Dior would delegate eight models and four dressers (Alla would never travel without Paulette, her favourite dresser), as well as the Marquis de Maussabré and Monsieur Donati, who were in charge of publicity. On these trips, she sometimes showed a real sense of humour. In 1951, during a trip to Brazil, a local millionaire, whose Latin temperament was obvious to everyone, fell madly in love with both the supermodels, Alla and Sylvie! This South American Croesus, convinced that his money made him irresistible, invited them to visit a famous jeweller's shop and choose whatever they liked. Once there, they scorned rubies and diamonds, and pointed to a little medal showing a saint. There was an outburst of laughter and the humiliated suitor vanished. But things were not always so pleasant: there were times when she could be very disagreeable. Once, in Greece, during a show for the King and Queen, the announcer could not perform, so the Marquis de Maussabré had to call out the names of the dresses himself, as was customary. Of course, he knew nothing about the job, and everyone did their best to help him — except Alla. Before she made her first appearance in the salon, he asked her, with his usual mild manner, to identify herself — meaning, of course, to give him the name of her dress. Alla understood the question perfectly well, but exclaimed indignantly: 'What! Do you mean you've forgotten? It's Alla, of course.'

And, without a further glance, she strode off, leaving the poor man to cope as best he could.

After the couturier's death, Alla continued to show Dior collections for Yves Saint Laurent. But when he had to leave, her status as star model was dangerously vulnerable. A new era began with the arrival of Marc Bohan, and she didn't really belong to it. At the end of the last collection which she showed in the Avenue Montaigne, the audience rose to give her an enthusiastic ovation. With her, the golden age of one of the most prestigious Parisan fashion houses ended. Shortly afterwards, Victoire (who was then star model at Saint Laurent) brought her in for several seasons, but she never really regained her former glory. Moreover, she did not have a stable private life which she could turn to. She had married Mike de Dulmen, a Polish count who had taken up photography and who gave her a son; but she had never truly got over her unhappy love affair with the great photo reporter Robert Capa, whom she had met in 1948 when he was making a short film about the haute couture collections. Capa was the epitome of the hypersensitive adventurer, who had never recovered from the tragic death of his wife, a young photographer of unparalleled beauty who was crushed by a tank during the Spanish Civil War. He was unable to give Alla the stability she needed. She spent the last years of her life between France and Italy, allowing herself to be slowly destroyed by alcoholism — a legacy of her Capa years — which she would not try to overcome. The funeral of Monsieur Dior's Asian 'fairy' took place on March 8, 1989, at the Russian Orthodox church in Rue Daru.

Victoire

On July 8, 1953, at the presentation of his Autumn-Winter collection, Christian Dior baptized two new models: Denise became 'Mauviette' and Jeanne, 'Victoire'. Mauviette's name meant 'lark', but it was also familiarly used as a word for a 'sissy' or 'weakling'. It proved cruelly apt, in both the literal and figurative senses, because a season later she vanished without trace. She did not have the brilliance and personality needed to become a star. In the same period, Victoire had established herself as one of the most famous models in Paris. As Christian Dior wrote in his memoirs: 'Victoire triumphed, justifying the name I had given her.'

At sixteen, she had been following an art course, with the aim of studying at the Ecole des Arts Décoratifs. It was then that her friends, charmed by her dark, wild beauty, advised her to take up modelling. She was attracted by the idea and asked for advice from the painter Touchague, for whom she often used to pose. He was as enthusiastic about the plan as her other acquaintances and suggested that she meet one of his friends, Michel de Brunhoff, the brains behind *Vogue* France, who would give her a letter of recommendation to the leading Parisian couturiers. This new acquaintance could hardly have been more encouraging: 'Go and see Christian Dior; he has been looking out for his 'rare bird' to turn up, so he is expecting you.'

In June, 1953, Jeanne came to the Avenue Montaigne, torn between hope and anxiety. As soon as he saw her, Christian Dior hired her without even reading the letter of recommendation that she had given him. He was at once taken by her natural, youthful charm. Her mischievous face recalled Leslie Caron in *An American in Paris,* her figure suggested a girl from the cellar bars in Saint Germain des Prés. She was short (Victoire was still a growing teenager, and during her years with Dior put on another four centimetres before reaching her full adult height), but with perfect measurements. In a word, she was the ideal model for Dior, different in every respect from those he already had working for him. She went against all the norms for haute couture: her sensual elegance and her perfectly shaped bosom would inspire some daring creations. It was on Victoire that Dior developed the first examples of what the British and American press called 'The Busty Look'.

He quickly decided to give her one or two outfits to wear for the forthcoming press show, but as the fittings went on, he realized that she was becoming a star. Eventually he decided to let her wear the three most characteristic designs of the new collection: 'Victorine', 'Coupole' and 'Télévision', as well as the key item in the show, the wedding dress. It was a move likely to arouse some envy. Few of those around the couturier could understand his enthusiasm for the young woman — starting with the models who, except for the adorable Renée, would not even speak to her. There was even more virulent criticism after Victoire's first show, with most of the clients also shouting their indignation. Apart from a few of the couturier's friends, like Mitza Bricard, Marie-Louise Bousquet and Carmen Baron

(Balthus' model), everyone wanted her to go. But Christian Dior, convinced that she had an innate sense of what was needed, refused to give way and insisted on using her for a further collection. Once more, his famous intuition had not let him down. After her next show, the élite of Parisian society was swearing by her.

In a few weeks, Victorine came to symbolize a new generation of models. After the vogue for women as sophisticated and ethereal objects, the fashion world fell for women as subjects — free, determined and bent on living their lives as they wanted. To illustrate this new trend, the fashion editors of the great women's magazines turned to Victoire, and she appeared frequently in the pages of *Vogue*, *Harper's* and *Elle*, photographed by Henry Clarke, Hiro or William Klein. But she preferred the atmosphere at the Avenue Montaigne to the work of a photographic model: the fitting sessions where calm and silence suddenly gave way to feverish, bubbling activity; the choice of materials; the minute process of creating each dress; the rehearsals just before a presentation for the press. Nothing could replace that excitement. Having become a key figure at Dior's, she enjoyed every kind of success: there were trips abroad, meetings with famous people, great balls and television shows. In 1956, she was even elected by the pupils at the Ecole Polytechnique to be 'godmother' to an entire student year. When she appeared in a uniform specially created for her by Christian Dior, she won everyone's vote.

She had liked Yves Saint Laurent ever since he first arrived at Dior in 1955. At that time, he was just an apprentice designer, unknown and shy, while Victoire was the star of the house, adulated and demanded by everyone. However, a deep affection soon grew up between them based on shared confidences and a sense of humour. For Yves, she was the ideal woman, with an insolent beauty that combined elegance and spontaneity, while always demonstrating wit and humour. He was reassured by her continual strength, which complemented his natural sensitivity. When Christian Dior died in 1957, and Yves Saint Laurent followed him as head of the fashion house, Victoire did a great deal to give him confidence and allow him to work in a calmer frame of mind. On January 15, 1958, the presentation of his first collection for Dior, the 'Trapeze Line', was an enormous success — so much so that on March 1, he agreed to pose with Victoire (wearing the wedding dress of this very latest look) for the cover of *Paris Match*. The photo, by Willy Rizzo, is now considered an historic document. It is also pleasant to know that Victoire did not only play the bride for the sake of a magazine. Barely a month later, she married Roger Thérond at the town hall of the 17th arrondissement of Paris, wearing a trapeze dress. The young couple's witnesses were Gaston Bonheur and Yves Saint Laurent. Victoire and Yves: they were to be a pair as famous as Pierre Balmain and Praline, 'Mademoiselle' Chanel and Marie-Hélène Arnaud, or Pierre Cardin and Hiroko Matsumoto. The relationship was a sensual osmosis, disturbing and ambiguous, which gave birth to unforgettable clothes. Such were the talent of the prodigy and the status of his supermodel that the house of Dior organized a show on November 11, 1958 at Blenheim Palace, Woodstock, in the presence of Princess Margaret: 133 dresses packed in seventeen trunks, and all insured for 150 million francs: a major expedition! At the end of the show, which was warmly applauded, the Duke of Marlborough told Yves Saint Laurent that to his mind Victoire was the Princess' double — which, from him, was the finest of compliments!

Their friendship was equally strong in times of good fortune as in more difficult periods. In July 1959, the new Autumn-Winter collection in which Saint Laurent presented (with other novelties) his 'Chinese lantern' (*lampion*) skirts, had a very mixed reception. The little world of fashion, which is by its very nature shifting, can hate as easily as it loves. Here, the young model's affection was a great help to him. Despite that, no collection had ever been more seductive in its originality — one has only to see the photos of Victoire taken by Irivng Penn and published in *Vogue* France, where she is wearing the characteristic dresses of this very individual line. Since then, time has dealt more justly with Yves Saint Laurent, since the collection is now rightly considered to be one of his most imaginative.

In September 1960, he had to enlist and do his compulsory military service. After a few weeks, he succumbed to a nervous breakdown and was discharged, but quickly realized that he had been replaced at the head of Dior by Marc Bohan. Consequently, with the support of his friends Victoire and Pierre Bergé, he decided to open his own fashion house. Even now, Victoire still remembers with emotion the months of uncertainty and anxiety that preceded the presentation of the first Saint Laurent collection in January 1962. She tried by every means possible to help her friend, refusing to lose hope. Thus, at the start of 1961, for the marriage of Philippine de Rothschild, a friend of the model's, he created a dress in pink chiffon hemmed with ostrich feathers. It was his first personal success, leading to the first photographs. Then, a little later, in July, Victoire and Zizi Jeanmaire, another of the young designer's greatest fans, posed for *Paris Match* in several of his creations. Finally there was a providential meeting with an American banker, J. M. Robinson, who became a sponsor. The foundations of the edifice were in place. The collection, shown at 30 bis, Rue Spontini, on January 29, 1962, was a triumph.

For Yves Saint Laurent, Victoire was much more than just a supermodel. From the moment his fashion house opened, he appointed her director of the salon and put her in charge of recruiting models. For the first show, she made a wise choice of the six young women who were to present the hundred or so outfits in the collection. The *cabine* consisted of a Russian, Deborah; two English girls, Morva and Heather; a Swiss, Françoise; a Eurasian, Fidélia; and finally a French girl, Paule de Mérindol, whom she had taken away from Chanel. As for Victoire herself, she always wore the couturier's finest designs. For his second collection, he gave her as many as twenty-seven. One need only recall her appearance in an evening coat entirely covered in white camellias, to understand how perfectly she fulfilled her role as the designer's muse. She also inspired the famous heart of precious stones, in diamonds and rubies, which became his good luck charm.

Victoire remained Yves Saint Laurent's muse and confidante, as well as his most valued assistant, until 1964. She had spent ten years in the world of haute couture, with all the passionate and emotionally fraught relationships that it could create between beings as rich and complex as Victoire and Yves Saint Laurent: 'We in every way resembled *enfants terribles,* at the same time

inseparable from one another and prisoners of our affection,'
she recalls. Now she felt an insurmountable need for something
new. Like so many other great models, she might have attempted to make a career in the cinema: she had plenty of
offers, each more attractive than the last. Gérard Oury even
invited her to take the lead in his film *La Main chaude*; but
Victoire had other plans which, to her mind were more attractive. As a reaction against the over-sophisticated clothes that she
had been more or less obliged to wear for all those years, she
decided to launch her own label. Throughout the world, the
second half of the 1960s saw a revolution in ready-to-wear,
thanks to designers like Emmanuelle Khanh and the Jacobsons
in France, Mary Quant in Great Britain, and Rudi Gernreich
and Betsey Johnson in the United States. All, in their own way,
managed to create a style that was really suited to the needs of
the young women of the new generation who did not want to
dress like their mothers. The mini-skirt, Lurex, metallic leather,
Rhodoid and Op Art prints were all the rage. Victoire, together
with Evelyne Prouvost, designed leotards, mini-dresses and
maxi-pullovers to wear with black patent leather thigh boots,
for the American chainstore J. C. Penney. Her personal style
was so successful, that she was asked to orchestrate the sixteenth
of the famous Franco-American balls, 'April in Paris' at the
Waldorf Astoria, New York, on the theme of 'Snow and Sun'.
She had her own models, wearing 'snowflake' hats designed by
the sculptor Marty, while she herself dressed the singer Mireille
Mathieu and the Olympic skier Marielle Goitschel, who had
been invited by the organizing committee to promote France.
Almost thirty years later, Victoire now laughs and regrets that
she went into styling. In her view, this period in the history of
fashion was destructive and responsible for a great deal of
ugliness, intentional or otherwise.

In 1971, after her second marriage to the painter Pierre
Doutreleau in January the previous year, she retired to devote
her time to her family and to bringing up her two sons, Mathias
and Ludovic. Today, Victoire divides her time between Switzerland, Paris and the South of France, while writing her memoirs,
which are eagerly awaited.

The Marc Bohan Period

Liane

Paris, October 1962. The last Thursday in the month, at the salon of Nina Ricci. On the advice of the head of a school of deportment where she was preparing to enrol, Anne-Marie had at last made up her mind to come to the Rue des Capucines. Nina Ricci, famous throughout the world for its clothes and for its perfumes, chief of all *L'Air du Temps*, was on the point of renewing its *cabine* of models. On the following day, she was asked to 'present' a shocking pink suit, with a large beige straw hat, in front of Jules-François Crahay, the official stylist of the firm. He examined her closely and eventually asked, in a kindly voice: 'What is your name, Mademoiselle?'

'Anne-Marie.'

'What a coincidence! That just happens to be the name of your dress. I hope it will bring you luck. You're hired.'

The word 'luck' was well-chosen. At 700 francs a month, together with one outfit from each collection and a free beauty treatment per season, she was delighted. Later, she bought the pink dress which had allowed her to become for two decades one of the greatest models in Paris.

For Anne-Marie, the rarefied atmosphere of a fashion house was something quite new. After finishing school, she had been successively apprentice in a leather goods shop, then a salesgirl and a window dresser. Naturally sensitive to refinement and beauty, she was soon encouraged wherever she went until she had the rare privilege, for a beginner, of being invited to Nina Ricci's at Milly-la-Forêt. On the other hand, Crahay perfectly understood her personality and would seldom give her 'sporty' outfits, which were not really suitable to her type of beauty. She was tall, very thin, with skin as white as porcelain and huge green eyes which, with her ebony black hair, undoubtedly suggested extreme sophistication. As a result Anne-Marie would have priority when it came to the most 'dressy' models, with a special preference for evening wear. At her first press show in January 1963, she presented the twenty most warmly applauded designs in the collection, including the wedding dress, which is always highly coveted. In a single show she had established herself as the star of the salon; it was, to say the least, an exceptional beginning.

When she heard that Crahay was leaving, Anne-Marie too decided to go. Although she was very happy at being taken on at once by Yves Saint Laurent, she could not resist the temptation of applying to Dior, where they were also looking for new models. She was precisely the kind of elegant, 'thoroughbred' woman who had contributed so much to the fame of the salon. Her arrival at Dior's was the most important moment in her career.

Throughout the five years that she spent in the Avenue Montaigne, she would always present between twenty-six and twenty-eight outfits per show. She had a perfect understanding with Marc Bohan, the man in charge. And it was he who persuaded her to change her first name. Leafing through the pages of a dictionary, she happened to come across the word 'Liane'. She immediately chose it.

'It suits you perfectly,' Bohan said to her, pleased with her decision. 'Tall and slim as you are, you couldn't find anything better.'

There was no doubt about her status as a supermodel. Of course, the inevitable corollary of this privilege was intense and continual work. She often stayed very late at night, until Bohan was entirely satisfied. Liane still remembers one fitting, only four days before the clothes were shown to the press: the couturier was putting the final touches to a short dress with yellow sequins, when he suddenly decided to make the same model, in the same material, but long and in pale pink. No sooner said than done. Liane left the studio at dawn. This kind of impulse was very common; and the new dress, it goes without saying, was magnificent. At the time of the collections, everyone hurried to the Avenue Montaigne. Liane paraded in front of Queen Fabiola, Princess Grace, Sophia Loren, the Duchess of Windsor, the Vicomtesse de Ribes and Rose Kennedy. She even once shared a taxi with the dowager Kennedy on coming out of a show. These encounters made for unforgettably magic moments.

Thanks to Dior, Liane went several times around the world, since the house organized three or four trips a year, each lasting one or two weeks. Every detail was planned out with military precison. For her first trip, a large-scale tour of Japan, Liane was accompanied by nine other models, Marc Bohan, the head of the haute couture department, the press and publicity officer and the *chef de cabine* — not to mention the 'treasure chests', meticulously sealed, each containing the dresses from the very latest collection. In Tokyo they were given star treatment: mobbed by photographers and overwhelmed with bouquets of flowers, chauffer-driven limousines, interpreters, press conferences, invitations, formal dinners, a parade for Princess Takamatsu and — as a bonus — a mild earthquake!

The job also took her to many other equally unforgettable cities: to Warsaw, where she saw her photograph, three and a half metres high, plastered on the walls of the Polish capital; to Athens, where after an evening in the port of Piraeus, the French ambassador Jacques Baeyens threw her fully clothed into a swimming pool; Madrid, where she was courted by

Alfonso de Bourbon-Dampierre, Duke of Cadiz; California, where she met Elizabeth Taylor and Richard Burton; Montreal, which she visited on board the famous liner 'France', with the witty Peter Ustinov as a fellow-passenger; and Iran, where she went for the coronation, because the future shahbanu had chosen Dior to design her ceremonial robes, and Liane was to present them. The princesses and the ladies in waiting were also in dresses by Bohan. It was a fantastic kaleidoscope of images, colours and emotions.

Later, when she became a freelance model, she travelled for Balmain, Lanvin and Léonard with the same enjoyment, always trying to avoid the usual, so-called 'unmissable', tourist attractions. In fact, this sometimes led her into quite dangerous situations. Once, in one of the riskier quarters of Nairobi, she saw a man being stabbed to death, ignored by the other passersby.

Little by little, Marc Bohan's style developed. He started to prefer smaller women, more natural and more approachable, with short hair and an androgynous appearance. After five years of happiness at Dior's, Liane had to leave. She worked successively for Hubert de Givenchy and Jean-Louis Scherrer, but she only really recovered her position as a supermodel when she went to Chanel's at the request of Lilou Marquand. Liane loved 'Mademoiselle', and even had the exceptional favour of being greeted by her with open arms at her villa in Lausanne. Indeed, she was the last model with whom Gabrielle Chanel worked, two days before her death. After that, Liane stayed with the firm until June 1974, when she decided to do only freelance work.

In 1982, after twenty years, Liane retired, with no regrets. She belonged to a generation of models who had the right to two haute couture oufits per collection and whose simple first name was a reference to most of the great couturiers. When she gave up her career, the word 'sophistication' had lost all meaning and the 'girls' had to be satisfied with cut-price boutique outfits! In these circumstances, it was better to quit. Five years later, when she was expecting her second child, she was asked to write her memoirs, which were published in 1977 as *Mannequin haute couture.* Liane had spoken a great deal, over many years, with the couturiers and the staff of the fashion houses. She had learned to look and listen, and her insight into all aspects of the business was exceptionally valuable. In her book, she describes what she remembers, leaving nothing out: shows, travel, meetings with people and also the hypocrisy and cruelty which are inherent in the world of haute couture. Now, having been free for more than ten years from any professional obligation, Liane devotes herself entirely to bringing up her three children, Laurent-David, Deborah and Audrey, whom she has from her marriage with the industrialist Edmond Cohen.

Jeanne Lanvin-Antonio del Castillo

Jeanne Lanvin, who began as an apprentice seamstress with Suzanne Talbot, became famous after the First World War for her so-called 'style' outfits, inspired by the pannier dresses of the eighteenth century. It was the antithesis of the 'Tomboy' look which was all the rage at the time. Jeanne was a much-admired couturier, decorator (she launched 'Lanvin blue', fitting out of the Théâtre Daunou), art collector and, of course, a creator of perfumes: *My Sin* (1925), *Arpège* (1927), *Sandal* (1931), *Rumeur* (1934) and *Prétexte* (1937) were all enormously successful. In 1960, fourteen years after Jeanne Lanvin's death, the house launched a new perfume, *Crescendo.*

Much influenced by the personality of her daughter, Marie-Blanche de Polignac, a musician and a great friend of the composer Nadia Boulanger, Jeanne dressed the poet Anna de Noailles and the actress Yvonne Printemps, among the cultural and social élite of Paris between the wars. All her clients loved her cleverly embroidered, low-waisted evening dresses, with their full ankle-length skirts.

When she died in 1946, her daughter took charge of the family empire. Four years later, Spanish couturier Antonio del Castillo was chosen as artistic director. Since 1945 he had been designing the Elizabeth Arden haute couture collections in New York and was able to preserve the ' Lanvin style', with its delicate classicism, while adding a note of very Spanish verve which can be seen, for example in his excessive taste for lace. This reached such a point that one day, when the management was asking him to offer more practical and wearable outfits, such as sports wear, he agreed with more or less good grace but added, with a sigh: 'Even so, it would be so much prettier in lace'.

After he left, in 1963, he was followed by personalities as different as Jules-François Crahay, bearing the prestige of his success with Nina Ricci; Maryll Lanvin, former supermodel and wife of Bernard Lanvin; Claude Montana, the most visionary of all French designers; and finally Dominique Morlotti, famous for his 'Christian Dior Monsieur' designs. The year 1993 was a turning point for Lanvin, because the new management decided temporarily to give up the 'haute couture' department and concentrate its activities on ready-to-wear. This decison vividly illustrates the spectacular difficulties currently facing the Parisian fashion houses.

Viviane Porte-Deblème

Between 1958 and 1968, Viviane Porte-Deblème was the star of the Castillo shows for Lanvin (up to 1963), then from 1964 onwards showing her own label, while at the same time one of the busiest freelance models of her generation. From Pierre Balmain to Philippe Venet, all the great couturiers called on her, at some time or another, to represent them. She could also be seen in the pages of *Harper's Bazaar* and *Vogue*, photographed by Avedon, Faurer or Hiro, as well as on American television in commercials for such leading firms as Revlon. Rarely has any model been so much in demand.

At eighteen years old, Viviane started out as an assistant buyer in the Galeries Lafayette. Here, a photographer from the Studio Harcourt, on the ground floor, asked her to pose for him. This was the young woman's first experience of modelling.

Only a few days later, Viviane's photographs were chosen to be used on a poster which would be displayed everywhere on the walls of the store for the Christmas season. Her first husband, delighted by the success of this advertising campaign, suggested that she continue along the same lines by applying to a fashion house. She seemed made for the job. Although she didn't like the idea of spending less time with her son Frédéric, Viviane followed his advice. Balmain and Heim found her too inexperienced to join their teams; they asked her to wait a little. It was then that she had the notion of going to Lanvin's, where the two official assisant designers, Philippe Guibourgé and Dominique Toubeix, helped her to prepare before she was introduced to Antonio del Castillo, the house stylist since 1950. When she finally entered the salon, Castillo, who was in a foul mood having just dismissed a model who had been one of his favourites for seven years, immediately softened: 'I love the way you carry your head! Stay with us!' Of Antonio del Castillo's assistants, the one Viviane most liked was Oscar de La Renta. 'He's superb, talented, adorable, a real gentleman. He was a wonderful friend and the memory of knowing him is the best thing I have from my years in the business.'

Although Viviane had only been taken on the week before the show for the new collection, the couturier decided to give her ten dresses or so to wear — a tribute to the instinctive confidence he had in her. A season later, as with every subsequent show in which she was to take part, he was entrusting her with twenty-five to thirty outfits. From the start of their professional relationship, they understood one another without needing to speak and she quickly became his favourite colleague. Castillo spoke a mixture of French and Spanish which was incomprehensible even to those closest to him, although no one would have dared ask him to repeat something that he had just said. Only Viviane was completely accustomed to his manner of communicating, so she could serve as an interpreter between the 'Master' and the rest of the world, thus earning the eternal gratitude of the rest of the staff.

They were so close that Castillo wanted no one except her at each press show to wear 'Granada', his 'lucky' outfit, which was always one of his famous dresses in Chantilly lace. It was like

Mademoiselle Chanel's 'No 5' or the heart made of precious stones for Yves Saint Laurent. Throughout their Lanvin years, Viviane wore his most inspired designs, including the 'goutte d'eau' dresses from the Autumn-Winter collection, 1960-1961, with their tiny bust ending high on a tight waist above a pear-shaped skirt. But their relationship was not limited to work. The designer often invited her to dinner at his Charles IV style apartment in the Rue de Constantine, as well as to his house in Valdemoro in Spain.

When Castillo opened his own salon in 1963, thanks to financial support from friends like Gloria Guinness and Barbara Hutton, Viviane did not hesitate for a moment before agreeing to go with him. In the next four years, touched by her friendship and loyalty, he surpassed himself for the sake of his protégée. She was also as good at presenting designs which combined two types of garment, and which he had already experimented on successfully at Lanvin's, such as the 'dress-coats', the 'trouser-skirt' or the 'dress-suits', as well as 'dalmatian' or 'aquarium' prints, his first asymetrically coiled evening dresses, 'patio dresses' and 'bistro dresses' which, in the designer's own words, were intended for dusk. But if one was to recall only one of Viviane's appearances in a Castillo dress, it would undoubtedly be the 'invisible blue' organza evening dress, embroidered with ten thousand pearls.

After a year and a half of exclusive work for Lanvin, while still remaining loyal to Antonio del Castillo, Viviane wanted to give up working for just one fashion house. Rather than see her leave for good, the couturier accepted any conditions she wished to impose: an understanding, a contract for ten days (the press show together with the nine following days for the buyers) and, finally, her only obligatory attendance, a month and a half of fittings before the collection — but only in the mornings! Meanwhile, she would retain her right to the privilege of keeping one design per collection, as well as her supermodel's salary. With this timetable, she was suddenly free for most of the year. In the tiny world of Parisian hatue couture, news travels very fast. Viviane, admired by everyone as Castillo's chief inspiration, was instantly in demand by other designers, and by the Chamber of Commerce. For the latter, Viviane travelled all around the world, thanks to the famous Baroness Dangel, who was in charge of organizing foreign events. Of course, she represented Lanvin and Castillo, but also Christian Dior (for whom she never worked in Paris), Hubert de Givenchy and Philippe Venet. Some couturiers, like Jacques Griffe, Guy Laroche, Mademoiselle Carven, Pierre Balmain and Mademoiselle Chanel, would ask for her for a press show, photographs or a television appearance. Still others (among them Madame Grès) waited for Viviane to be free of all other engagements so that she could accompany them to New York or Gstaad for a show. But far from confining herself merely to haute couture, she also worked with famous hairdressers, including Alexandre and the Carita sisters, and with great furriers, such as Chombert, Kotler, Mendel and Révillon.

In the midst of this whirl of activity, Viviane also found time to become a photographic model. Diana Vreeland herself asked her, after a Lanvin show, to come to the United States to pose for *Harper's*. Once in New York, she was taken under contract by Plaza Five, the agency set up by Dovima. Not to be outdone by their famous rival, the editors of *Vogue* USA often called on her services. But Viviane far preferred the excitement of a show to the more static ambiance of a photographic studio, so when Dovima offered her work for television, at the request of Revlon and the great jewellers' shops on Fifth Avenue, she was delighted. This in itself gave her an especially close relationship with the American fashion industry. In 1965 she was even chosen Best Model of the Year at an award ceremony in Las Vegas, which gives some measure of her popularity in that country.

Like a lot of great models, Viviane also had some experience in the cinema. She had always been compared to a French haute couture verson of Greta Garbo — so much so, in fact, that one photo of her, taken in a night club in New York, appeared the next day on the front page of a daily newspaper with the caption: 'Has Garbo got a daughter?' The divine Garbo was intrigued by the publicity and even invited Viviane to meet her! It is therefore not surprising that she was contacted by a Hollywood agent in 1961 to appear in a remake of *Back Street*, directed by David Miller and co-starring Susan Hayward and Vera Miles.

In 1968, the Chamber of Commerce asked her to replace Baroness Dangel. Viviane accepted without hesitation, intrigued by the idea of once more finding a new role. She organized prestige shows abroad, jointly with the Comité Colbert, and in Paris supervised the making of several films about haute couture. In her memoirs, *Mannequin haute couture,* Liane Viguié recalls a trip that she made, thanks to Viviane, to Argentina: 'Ten fashion houses were involved in the trip, each with a magnificent model at its head. Viviane has always had very fine taste, and each couturier was always very well represented when she chose a "freelance". She had tremendous class, real style, as they say, and she wanted the girls to be like her — not only beautiful, but with presence. I have often thought Viviane was like Garbo, a very special kind of beauty which you don't find round every corner. In my view, she was magnificent, *and* with a wit and a sense of fun and an inimitable, infectious laugh which added to her charm. This was our "master of ceremonies" for our trip to Buenos Aires.'

In 1973, at the birth of her twins, Léopold and Pierre-Edouard, from her second marriage to a dental surgeon, Viviane decided to leave the world of haute couture for a while. A little later, she began a career in fashion journalism, working for the magazine *Rare Choice,* while from time to time continuing to organize shows for her couturier friends. And finally, she has been giving lessons in 'style' every ten days at the spa resort of Contrexéville. One could not wish for a better teacher.

Selected Bibliography

Couturiers

General

Jouve, Marie-Andrée et Demornex, Jacqueline: *Balenciaga*, translated by Augusta Audubert, Thames and Hudson, London, 1988.

Marquand, Lilou: *Chanel m'a dit*, Ed. Jean-Claude Lattès, Paris, 1990.

Giroud, Françoise et Van Dorssen, Sacha: *Christian Dior*, translated by Stewart Spencer, Thames and Hudson, London, 1987.

Guillaume, Valérie: *Jacques Fath*, Ed. Paris-Musées/Adam Biro, Paris, 1993.

Pierre Balmain: 40 années de création, Musée de la Mode et du Costume, Palais Galliera, Ed. Paris-Musées, Paris, 1985.

Pierre Cardin Past Present and Future, with an introductory essay by Valerie Mendes, Dirk Nishen Publishing, London/Berlin, 1990.

Givenchy: 40 ans de création, Musée de la Mode et du Costume, Palais Galliera, Ed. Paris-Musées, Paris, 1991.

Couturiers on Themselves

Balmain, Pierre: *My Years and Seasons*, Doubleday, New York, 1965.

Dior, Christian: *Je suis couturier*, Ed. du Conquistador, Paris, 1951.

Dior, Christian: *Dior by Dior*, translated by Antonia Fraser, Weidenfeld and Nicolson, London, 1957.

Schiaparelli, Elsa: *Shocking Life*, (some pages on the postwar period), J.M. Dent & Sons, London, 1954.

Cover Girls and Supermodels

General

Castle, Charles: *Model Girl*, (from the turn of the century to the 1970s), David & Charles, Ltd, 1977.

Cover Girls and Supermodels on Themselves

Bettina: *Bettina par Bettina*, Ed. Flammarion, Paris, 1964.

Dawnay, Jean: *Model Girl*, Weidenfeld & Nicolson, London, 1956.

Freddy: *Dans les coulisses de la haute couture parisienne*, memoirs of a supermodel told to Jean Carlier, Ed. Flammarion, Paris, 1956.

Leigh, Dorian: *The Girl Who Had Everything*, (with Laura Hobe), Doubleday, New York, 1980.

Lucky: *Présidente Lucky, mannequin de Paris*, souvenirs recueillis par Odette Keyzin, Ed. Fayard, Paris, 1961.

Praline: *Praline mannequin de Paris*, Ed. du Seuil, Paris, 1951.

Shrimpton, Jean: *My Own Story: the Truth about Modelling*, Bantam Books, New York, 1965.

Shrimpton, Jean: *An Autobiography*, (with Unity Hall), Ebury Press, London, 1990.

Thurlow, Valerie: *Model in Paris*, Robert Hale, London, 1975.

Viguié, Liane: *Mannequin haute couture*, Ed. Robert Laffont, Paris, 1977.

Fashion Photographers

General

Devlin, Polly: *Vogue Book of Fashion Photography*, Thames and Hudson, London, 1979.

Harrison, Martin: *Appearances, Fashion Photography since 1949*, Cape, London, 1991.

Photographers

Avedon, Richard: *Photographs 1947-1977*, Thames and Hudson, London, 1978.

Beaton, Cecil: *Beaton in Vogue*, Thames and Hudson, London, 1986.

Dahl-Wolfe, Louise: *A Photographer's Scrap Book*, St Martin's/Marek, New York, 1984.

Lawford, Valentine: *Horst, his Work and his World*, Alfred A. Knopf, New York, 1984.

Parkinson, Norman: *Lifework*, Weidenfeld & Nicolson, London, 1983.

Penn, Irving: *Passage. A Work Record*, Cape, London, 1990.

Sieff, Jeanloup: *Demain le temps sera plus vieux*, photographs 1950-1990, Ed. Contrejour, Paris, 1990.

L'Elégance des années 50 photographiée par Henry Clarke, Ed. Herscher, Paris, 1986.

John French Fashion Photographer, compiled and edited by Valerie D. Mendes, published by The Victoria & Albert Museum, London, 1984.

World Press

Carter, Ernestine: *With Tongue in Chic*, Michael Joseph, London, 1974.

Woolman Chase, Edna et Chase, Ilka: *Always in Vogue*, Doubleday, New York, 1954.

Dubois-Jallais, Denise: *La Tzarine Hélène Lazareff et l'aventure de Elle*, Ed. Robert Laffont, Paris, 1984.

Snow, Carmel et Aswell, Mary: *The World of Carmel Snow*, McGraw-Hill Book Co, New York, 1962.

Vreeland, Diana: *D.V.*, Alfred A. Knopf, New York, 1984.

Index